British Theatre since 1955

OPUS General Editors
Keith Thomas *Humanities*
J. S. Weiner *Sciences*

Ronald Hayman

British Theatre since 1955

A Reassessment

WITHDRAWN

WITHDRAWN

Oxford University Press 1979

Oxford New York Toronto Melbourne

Oxford University Press, Walton Street, Oxford OX2 6DP

OXFORD LONDON GLASGOW
NEW YORK TORONTO MELBOURNE WELLINGTON
KUALA LUMPUR SINGAPORE JAKARTA HONG KONG TOKYO
DELHI BOMBAY CALCUTTA MADRAS KARACHI
NAIROBI DAR ES SALAAM CAPE TOWN

British Library Cataloguing in Publication Data

Hayman, Ronald
    British theatre since 1955.
    1. Theatre – Great Britain – History – 20th century
    I. Title
    792'.0941   PN2595   78–41091

    ISBN 0-19-219127-6
    ISBN 0-19-289113-8 Pbk

Printed in Great Britain by
Billing & Sons Limited, Guildford, London and Worcester

Contents

Acknowledgements

Thanks are due to Faber & Faber Ltd for permission to quote the line from T. S. Eliot's *Sweeney Agonistes* on p. 5, and also to the following publishers of plays quoted in passing: John Calder Ltd. (Howard Barker, Edward Bond: *Early Morning*); Calder & Boyars Ltd. (Heathcote Williams); Jonathan Cape Ltd. (Arnold Wesker); André Deutsch Ltd. (Peter Shaffer: *Equus*); Eyre Methuen Ltd. (John Arden, Edward Bond, Howard Brenton, David Edgar, Barrie Keeffe, David Mercer, John Mortimer, Joe Orton, Harold Pinter, Stephen Poliakoff, Charles Wood); Faber & Faber Ltd. (Samuel Beckett, Trevor Griffiths, David Hare, Peter Nichols, John Osborne, Tom Stoppard); Hamish Hamilton Ltd. (Peter Shaffer: *The Royal Hunt of the Sun*); Heinemann Educational Ltd. (John Whiting).

I'd also like to express my thanks to Catharine Carver, whose editorial help is so much more than editorial help.

R.H.

Introduction

This book is more critical than historical. If, in the space at my disposal, I had tried to offer a panoramic survey of theatrical achievement since 1955, I would have written only a superficial summary, like a distended encyclopedia article. I have not tried to avoid wide-angle-lens generalizations, but I have combined them with close-up examination of certain playwrights and certain plays. So many journalistic valuations pass into critical currency that what is needed, I think, is a reassessment based on criteria that are neither those of the reviewer nor those of the literary critic. I have tried in this book to give my own answer to the question 'How much has been achieved in the British theatre since *Waiting for Godot* had its London premiere in 1955?' The answer, of course, must take account of non-literary achievement—creativity in the use of theatrical space, the development of new rapport with the audience, the use of improvisation, and so on. There is still not enough interpenetration between the work of writer, director, and actors, but there is more than there has ever been before, and this is itself an important achievement.

I have ignored most of the playwrights who made their main contribution before 1955—Noël Coward, J. B. Priestley, Terence Rattigan, Ben Travers, and Christopher Fry, for instance. Other omissions, like the plays of E. A. Whitehead, Peter Terson, and Snoo Wilson, are more arbitrary, but I prefer to cover a limited area fairly thoroughly, rather than deal perfunctorily with everything that has a claim to consideration. This is why I have made no attempt to cover the complete works of each playwright I discuss. David Hare bulks quite large in this book, but I have said what I want to say about him by concentrating on *Teeth 'n'*

Smiles and *Plenty*, barely mentioning *Fanshen* and ignoring *Slag, Knuckle*, and *The Great Exhibition.*

The three chapters about playwrights have grown out of an attempt to answer three groups of questions which seem important. The first is about language and the quality of the writing. Can a good playwright be a bad writer? How well-written are the sentences that constitute the dialogue of Pinter, Osborne, Arden, Bond, and Stoppard? The first chapter takes its perspective from T. S. Eliot, who understood that the problem of language was crucial, though he did not realize how clearly he had polarized the alternatives in his pre-war verse. In *The Waste Land* (1922) and in *Sweeney Agonistes* (1932) there are passages of highly rhythmic, highly stylized imitations of working-class speech. In *The Waste Land* these are juxtaposed, effectively, against passages written in a complex literary language. In all his plays except *Sweeney* Eliot opted for a literary language, making larger and progressively more disastrous compromises in his attempts at approximating to conversational English. He left it for Pinter and subsequent playwrights to explore the possibilities of uneducated speech. But how much has been lost in the process of eliminating the kind of consciousness that can be expressed only in more complex language? And how completely has it been eliminated?

The second group of questions is about innovation. Chauvinistically, we usually assume that British playwrights have contributed more than any others to contemporary drama. Numerically the British team is very strong, but is any of our playwrights comparable as an innovator to Beckett, Ionesco, Genet, or Peter Handke? How much is there in contemporary British drama that is genuinely new, and how much does it matter if there is little? This question is not altogether separate from the question of language and the quality of the writing, but it is convenient to treat it separately, though some of the dramatists considered from this point of view have already featured in the first chapter.

A few of them recur in the third chapter, which is about political theatre. Before 1955 very few of our playwrights were interested in using theatre as a means of political persuasion, but this is now the dominant motive for some of our most successful and most interesting writers. The question of how far they have succeeded in writing good plays is not entirely separate from either of the first two questions. Didacticism tends to inhibit both experiment and concern for good writing. The playwright who is urgently concerned to convert or to polemicize needs to express himself clearly and forcefully, but he does not usually have time to worry about form or phrasing.

The last chapter is about new configurations within the play, within the playhouse, and in the relationship between performance and public. Visual and physical elements in the play have become less subservient to verbal elements. In the theatre much less depends on illusion. There has been a strong reaction against the rigidity that the proscenium imposes on the relationship between acting area and auditorium. The tendency has been towards inviting the audience to be less passive and to become more involved in what is more obviously a game. Of the four areas this is the one in which it is hardest to evaluate what has been achieved. In itself the new flexibility is admirable and, used imaginatively, it can give great stimulus to the audience's imagination. This, unfortunately, seldom happens.

1 The quality of the writing

At the beginning of the Fifties it was plausibly being argued that the best hopes for the future of the English theatre lay in the possibility of a reunion between poetry and drama in plays like Christopher Fry's *The Lady's Not for Burning* (1948) and T. S. Eliot's *The Cocktail Party* (1949). 'Poetry is the language of reality,' declared Fry in a 1950 radio talk, while Eliot said: 'If the poetic drama is to reconquer its place, it must, in my opinion, enter into overt competition with prose drama.'[1]

As a poet T. S. Eliot had learned much from Elizabethan and Jacobean dramatists; as a critic he had been preoccupied with verse drama since 1919. In 1928 he was arguing that 'The human soul, in intense emotion, strives to express itself in verse. . . . The tendency, at any rate, of prose drama is to emphasize the ephemeral and superficial; if we want to get at the permanent and universal we tend to express ourselves in verse.'[2] More recently George Steiner has made a similar point: 'How could Hemingway's language convey the inward life of more manifold or articulate characters? Imagine trying to translate the consciousness of Raskolnikov into the vocabulary of "The Killers". . . . The brute snobbish fact is that men who die speaking as does Macbeth are more tragic than those who sputter platitudes in the style 6f Willy Loman.'[3] The prose of contemporary drama is almost as remote from the prose of Dostoevsky as from the verse of Shakespeare. How are we to measure the work of Pinter, Osborne, or Stoppard against the standard that

[1] 'Poetry and Drama', *Selected Prose* (1953), p. 79.
[2] 'A Dialogue on Dramatic Poetry', *Selected Essays* (1932; 3rd edn., 1951), p. 46.
[3] 'The Retreat from the Word' in *Language and Silence* (1967; Penguin edn., 1969), p. 51.

Steiner implies? How legitimate is it to ask whether the consciousness of Lear or Hamlet could be translated into the language of *The Caretaker*?

Eliot understood that the central problem facing the serious dramatist was the problem of language, but he might have become a better playwright if he had not turned his back so uncompromisingly on his first tentative attempt to solve the problem. In 1932 he had published a work he had abandoned without thinking it had any chance of being staged: *Sweeney Agonistes—Fragments of an Aristophanic Melodrama*. Using the uneducated speech of low-life characters, he imposed jazz rhythms on their repetitions, circumlocutions, and approximations:

> DORIS: I like Sam
> DUSTY: *I* like Sam
> Yes and Sam's a nice boy too.
> He's a funny fellow
> DORIS: He *is* a funny fellow
> He's like a fellow once I knew.
> *He* could make you laugh.
> DUSTY: Sam can make you laugh:
> Sam's all right
> DORIS: But Pereira won't do.
> We can't have Pereira
> DUSTY: Well what you going to do?

Today some of the dialogue may remind us of early Pinter, though the rhythms are stronger and the characters more self-conscious about the difficulty of communicating:

> I gotta use words when I talk to you
> But if you understand or if you don't
> That's nothing to me and nothing to you
> We all gotta do what we gotta do

Ten years earlier, using unrhymed dialogue, Eliot had written a comparable passage in *The Waste Land* (lines 139–72). There is only one speaker, a barmaid, and apart from shouting 'HURRY UP PLEASE ITS TIME' five times, her monologue consists almost entirely of quoted dialogue, and, as in *Sweeney*, the liveliness and tension of the writing depend not so much on accurate mimicry of the character's speech as on an intensity which derives from Eliot's mixture of fascination and revulsion:

> You have them all out, Lil, and get a nice set,
> He said, I swear, I can't bear to look at you.

Writing about Baudelaire in a 1930 essay Eliot said: 'It is not merely in the use of imagery of common life, not merely in the use of imagery of the sordid life of a great metropolis, but in the elevation of such imagery to the *first intensity*—presenting it as it is, and yet making it represent something much more than itself—that Baudelaire has created a mode of release and expression for other men.'[4] Among Baudelaire's images are prostitutes, mulattoes, hermaphrodites, corpses, shrouds, lice, and defecation, but his preoccupation, as Eliot says, was with the possibility of redemption and with the problem of good and evil. In the pub sequence of *The Waste Land* and in *Sweeney*, Eliot used the cliché-ridden language of prostitutes, procuresses, pimps, garrulous barmaids and newspaper reports on crime, and the tawdry imagery of false teeth, fortune-telling, and pills taken to induce abortions, but, like Baudelaire, he made squalor and evil flower into something beautiful. beautiful.

It was left for later playwrights to develop the mineral resources of the territory Eliot had pioneered. He rejected *Sweeney*, excluding it from the collection of his plays, making no reference to it in his retrospective comments on his development as a playwright,[5] and refusing to learn from his own experience. The principal characters in his later plays may be more articulate, and he tried to make them more complex, but they are less vivid. None of them is under-educated or underprivileged. The choruses in *Murder in the Cathedral* (1939) are spoken by the Women of Canterbury. But their language has nothing to do with that of their real-life equivalents.

Of the prose dramatists working in the Fifties the one

---

[4] 'Baudelaire', *Selected Essays*, p. 426.
[5] In 'Poetry and Drama', op. cit., and 'The Three Voices of Poetry', *On Poetry and Poets* (1957).

most deeply imbued with Eliot's influence was John Whiting. *Saint's Day*, which won the competition organized by the Arts Theatre for the 1951 Festival of Britain, was written chiefly as a technical exercise, and some of the long speeches sound like pastiche of Eliot:

> At one moment there is laughter and conversation and a progression: people move and speak smoothly and casually, their breathing is controlled and they know what they do. Then there occurs a call from another room, the realization that a member of the assembly is missing, the sudden shout into the dream and the waking to find the body with the failing heart lying in the corridor—with the twisted limbs at the foot of the stairs—the man hanging from the beam, or the child floating drowned in the garden pool.

John Whiting believed strongly that dramatic dialogue needed to be much richer in texture than what he called 'the direct unornamented speech of everyday life'. In a 1957 lecture on 'The Art of the Dramatist' he said:

> Pick up a conversation in the street and it may go something like this:
> 'Now look here I said I'm not having this I said and so he says What and I says I'm not having it I'm telling you I says up and down the stairs you were four times this morning telling him I was up and down I says in your boots with little Else trying to sleep oh I told him.'
> No, the direct unornamented speech of the theatre must be as artificial as any form.[6]

Kenneth Tynan treated the lecture to a disparaging review, sardonically comparing the playwright to 'some attenuated hermit saint bravely keeping his chin up while being sucked through the revolving doors of a holiday camp'. Tynan was right, though, to argue that, far from being drab and dull, the parody of uneducated speech was 'infectiously and rivetingly alive. One longed to hear more.'[7] But, like Eliot, Whiting left it for Pinter to give us more.

Even in Whiting's mature plays *Marching Song* (1954) and *The Devils* (1961) the dialogue is in line with Eliot's remarks in 'Poetry and Drama' about prose stylists such as Congreve and Shaw, in whose plays 'the prose in which the characters speak is as remote, for the best part, from the

---

[6] Reprinted in *On the Art of the Dramatist* (1970), p. 97.

[7] 'The Purist View', reprinted in *Curtains* (1961), pp. 166–7.

vocabulary, syntax and rhythm of our ordinary speech—
with its fumbling for words, its constant recourse to approximation, its disorder and its unfinished sentences—as
verse is.'[8] Whiting had no interest in experimenting with the
theatrical possibilities inherent in the fumblings of ordinary
speech, the constant recourse to approximation, the disorder, and the unfinished sentences. But Harold Pinter was
astute enough to realize that fumblings, approximations,
and syntactical muddles were innately theatrical.

Chekhov had taken advantage of the inconsequentiality
in casual conversation, but Pinter found a new way of ex-
tracting comedy from discontinuity, repetition, confusion,
and our habit of not attending to what other people are
saying:

> MR. KIDD: Hallo, Mr. Hudd, how are you, all right? I've been
> looking at the pipes.
> ROSE: Are they all right?
> MR. KIDD: Eh?
> ROSE: Sit down, Mr. Kidd.
> MR. KIDD: No, that's all right. I just popped in, like, to see how
> things were going. Well, it's cosy in here, isn't it?
> ROSE: Oh, thank you, Mr. Kidd.
> MR. KIDD: You going out today, Mr. Hudd? I went out. I came
> straight in again. Only to the corner, of course.
> ROSE: Not many people about today, Mr. Kidd.
> MR. KIDD: So I thought to myself, I'd better have a look at those
> pipes. In the circumstances. I only went to the corner, for a few necess-
> ary items. It's likely to snow. Very likely, in my opinion.
> ROSE: Why don't you sit down, Mr. Kidd?
> MR. KIDD: No, no, that's all right.

In this early sequence from his first play *The Room* (written
1957; produced by students 1957; professionally premiered
1960) Mr. Hudd remains puzzlingly silent while Rose and
Mr. Kidd fail to answer the questions they put to each
other, answering questions they don't put, repeating themselves and misunderstanding each other. Realistic though
the conversation is, its accuracy is quite unlike that of the
tape-recorder, containing, as it does, a strong element of
parody. As in *Sweeney*, the pattern is neither wholly im-

[8] *Selected Prose*, p. 68.

posed nor wholly discovered, but it is heightened. Against the perspective provided by Mr. Hudd's refusal to speak, we are invited to inspect the other two characters' inept, half-hearted attempts at communication; but dialogue does not seem to have the same function of establishing identity as in the conventional play. We are implicitly being asked to concentrate not so much on the individuals as on the way they talk, and on the discrepancy between the words they utter and the preoccupations that lie underneath.

Pinter's dialogue corresponds to his analysis (in a speech made in 1962) of what conversation is: 'The speech we hear is an indication of that we don't hear. It is a necessary avoidance, a violent, sly, anguished or mocking smokescreen which keeps the other in its place.'[9] One of the main sources of the intensity Pinter has often achieved is his alertness to the painful awkwardness of the dislocation between the two kinds of speech. Another source is his patterning, which tends to emphasize and even ritualize the rhythms in the repetitions.[10] Both patterning and dislocation push the dramatic dialogue away from the kind of articulacy typified by Raskolnikov and Macbeth, who always mean exactly what they say.

The paragon of articulacy in contemporary British drama is Jimmy Porter in *Look Back in Anger* (1956), but the success of that play depended on his being both more and less than an individual. Osborne was not trying to use his style of speaking as a means of characterizing him. Jimmy Porter is being offered as a spokesman for a disaffected generation whose response to the play might be comparable with that of its American counterpart to the James Dean film *Rebel Without a Cause* (1955). Jimmy Porter's speeches were contrived to express the misgivings, the grievances, and the impatience of almost everyone who resented the power and the corruption of parents, Establishment politicians, and

[9] Reprinted in *Plays: One* (1976).
[10] Cf. Andrew K. Kennedy, *Six Dramatists in Search of a Language* (1975), p. 177.

anyone with power, anyone who in 1956 could be blamed for the way Britain was drifting. Without being a revolutionary, Jimmy set himself up as a pugnacious enemy of the *status quo* and of the apathy it was floating on. 'Let's pretend that we're human beings,' he says, 'and that we're actually alive.' Thousands of people wanted to feel that, like Jimmy, they were full of febrile energy and immune to the endemic complacency. The question *Look Back in Anger* begs is the question of whether Jimmy is wasting his energy, haranguing only Cliff, Alison, and Helena, who are not going to be galvanized into action. But in so far as the stage is a platform, he is haranguing the audience. 'I want to make people feel,' Osborne said, 'to give them lessons in feeling.'[11]

The play has dated rather badly, partly because of its topical references. More important, the actual texture of the writing is loose, often journalistic, and sometimes jokey. Some of the invective is powerful and amusing, especially when it is turned outwards to public events, but when Jimmy's speeches become introspective, they are embarrassingly sentimental and self-approving:

Was I really wrong to believe that there's a—a kind of—burning virility of mind and spirit that looks for something as powerful as itself? The heaviest, strongest creatures in this world seem to be the loneliest.

Even in *The Entertainer* (produced 1957), which is better written and more tightly constructed, the effectiveness of the rhetoric depends very much on the actors:

I think you really feel something too, in spite of all that Trafalgar Square stuff. You're what they call a sentimentalist. You carry all your responses about with you, instead of leaving them at home. While everyone else is sitting on their hands you're the Joe at the back cheering and making his hands hurt. But you'll have to sit on your hands like everyone else. Oh, you think I'm just a tatty old music hall actor who should be told the truth, like Old Billy, that people don't wear sovereign cases and patent leather shoes any more. You know when you're up there you think you love all those people around you out there, but you don't. You don't love them, you're not going to stand up and make a beautiful fuss. If you learn it properly you'll get

[11] *Declaration: A Symposium*, ed. Tom Maschler (1958), p. 65.

yourself a technique. You can smile, darn you, smile, and look the friendliest jolliest thing in the world, but you'll be just as dead and smug and used up, and sitting on your hands just like everybody else. You see this face, you see this face, this face can split open with warmth and humanity. It can sing, and tell the worst, unfunniest stories in the world to a great mob of dead, drab erks and it doesn't matter, it doesn't matter. It doesn't matter because—look at my eyes. I'm dead behind these eyes. I'm dead, just like the whole inert, shoddy lot out there. It doesn't matter because I don't feel a thing, and neither do they. We're just as dead as each other.

Delivered by Laurence Olivier, this speech was extremely moving, but the sentences are not shaped or weighted to put the stress where it is needed. The syntax is slipshod, and the fumbling approximations are not put critically into focus. In context 'all that Trafalgar Square stuff' is comprehensible because of the earlier references to the rallies, but the definition of a sentimentalist is interesting neither in itself nor as a sidelight on Archie, while precision and incisiveness are equally lacking in the other observations. There is neither logical development nor pointed inconsequentiality in the argument, while the cliché phrases are neither being offered in inverted commas as clichés nor carrying the weight that is being placed on them.

But the play is enriched by the relationship it establishes with the music hall tradition. If Jimmy Porter's tirades had in many ways resembled the stand-up comedian's monologues, *The Entertainer* plugs itself firmly into a vaudeville power circuit. Unlike Eliot, Osborne was not too fastidious to take a coarse-grained art form as his model. Eliot had admired the comedienne Marie Lloyd and her 'capacity for expressing the soul of the people'. He said that 'no other comedian succeeded so well in giving expression to the life of that audience, in raising it to a kind of art.'[12] In his poetry Eliot was not above borrowing rhythms from jazz or the speech of low-life characters, but apart from *Sweeney* none of his dramatic writing tries to blend high art with low comedy.

---

[12] 'Marie Lloyd' (1923), *Selected Essays*, p. 457.

A closer approximation to a Shakespearian richness of texture is to be found in the work of John Arden, which always moves further away from naturalism and often moves back into history. 'People must want to come to the theatre *because* of the artificiality, not despite it,' he said in 1960. '. . . I am pleading for the revival of Poetic Drama, no less.'[13] Though his plays cannot be classified as verse drama, substantial sequences are written in rhyming verse, while much of the imagery in the prose is poetic. But, like Osborne and unlike Eliot, Arden has drawn on popular art forms. His main debt is to the ballads, and he allows their influence to permeate his language, his narrative, and his construction. The most ballad-like sequence in *Serjeant Musgrave's Dance* (produced 1959) comes near the end of the second act, when Annie, the barmaid, offers herself to each of the three soldiers who are sleeping in the stables. Each, in turn, rejects her:

ATTERCLIFFE: Now then, what'll I do to you, eh? How d'you reckon you're going to quench *me*? Good strong girly with a heart like a horse-collar, open it up and let 'em all in. And it still wouldn't do no good.

ANNIE (*hard and hostile*): Wouldn't it? Try.

ATTERCLIFFE: Ah, No. Not tonight. What would *you* know of soldiers?

ANNIE: More'n you'd think I'd know, maybe.

ATTERCLIFFE: I doubt it. Our Black Jack'd say it's not material. He'd say there's blood on these two hands. (*He looks at his hands with distaste.*) You can wipe 'em as often as you want on a bit o' yellow hair but it still comes blood the next time so why bother, *he'd* say. And *I'd* say it too. Here. (*He kisses her again and lets her go.*) There you are, girly: I've given you all you should get from a soldier. Say 'Thank you, boy', and that's that.

The simple poetic images contribute to the vigour and the appeal of the writing, but, like the movement of the scene from one refusal to the next, the movement of the dialogue would be more acceptable in a ballad. Arden's indictment of military butchery depends on characterizing the sergeant and his men as caught in an uncomfortable tension between morbid guilt and repentant evangelism, but it is very hard to

[13] *New Theatre Magazine*, vol. I, no. 2 (1960).

believe that three hardened sex-starved soldiers would each reject a willing girl. Generally Arden was finding it difficult to distil his statement into theatrical action. Nearly all the best speeches directly explicate the play's central message. One example is the rhyming verse Annie declaims during her first confrontation with the soldiers:

> I'll tell you for what a soldier's good:
> To march behind his roaring drum,
> Shout to us all: 'Here I come
> I've killed as many as I could—
> I'm stamping into your fat town
> From the war and to the war
> And every girl can be my whore
> Just watch me lay them squealing down.'
> And that's what he does and so do we.
> Because we know he'll soon be dead
> We strap our arms round the scarlet red
> Then send him weeping over the sea.
> Oh he will go and a long long way.
> Before he goes we'll make him pay
> Between the night and the next cold day—
> By God there's a whole lot more I could say—
> What good's a bloody soldier 'cept to be dropped into a slit in the ground like a letter in a box.

Though the plot justifies her attitude by making her the ex-lover of a soldier who has been killed, the speech has scarcely anything more to do with her than it has with any of the other anti-war characters.

The most effective of them is Musgrave himself, but even with him it is obvious that message preceded character. 'I decided what he had to say, and why he had to say it, and roughly what he was going to do about it, before I worked out the character,' said Arden in an interview. 'The character came to fit the actions.'[14] Musgrave's rhetoric is at its best in the climactic denunciation of war when he is haranguing the crowd in the market square. Like Osborne in *The Entertainer*, Arden has his spokesman address the audience directly, while one of the soldiers trains a Gatling gun on the auditorium, enforcing an uncomfortable identification with the onstage crowd. Hauling up a skeleton in

---

[14] *Encore*, no. 32 (July–August 1961), p. 31.

tattered military uniform to display it like a flag on a pole, Musgrave breaks into verse—the stage direction requires him to sing—stamping out the rhythm in his fanatical dance:

> Up he goes and no one knows
> How to bring him downwards
> Dead man's feet
> Over the street
> Riding the roofs
> And crying down your chimneys
> Up he goes and no one knows
> Who it was that rose him
> But white and red
> He waves his head
> He sits on your back
> And you'll never never lose him
> Up he goes and no one knows
> How to bring him downwards.

As in Annie's speech, and as in the ballads, colours have a simple emblematic significance, the redness of the tunic merging with the redness of blood.

Armstrong's Last Goodnight (produced 1964) is a more ambitious piece of writing. The theme is extremely complex, but there are passages of balladlike simplicity in the dialogue. One of the characters is reminiscent of Annie—a girl whose lover has been killed. Grief-stricken, she has left home to lead a wild life in the forest. Conceived like a ballad character, she speaks ballad language:

> Are ye comen, my wearie dearie,
> Are ye comen, my lovely hinnie,
> I will find ye a wee bracken bush
> To keep the north wind frae aff your ancient body.

Lyrically pleasing though this is, ballad situations are stock situations, and stock situations encourage scamped motivations.

What is most impressive—and most Shakespearian—about the play is its success in using words and actions to build up a rugged sense of locale without needing any visual help from the set. No English playwright since Shakespeare can have made better or fuller use of a forest, with only the density of the language to suggest the density of the woodland, while the bleakness of the hills is evoked by stony words. When Wamphray dies, pinned against a tree by the spears of the Eliots, their leader's farewell is: 'He will remain here on this fellside for the better nourishment of the corbies. Ride.'

The play is indebted to the ballad 'Johnie Armstrang' for its inspiration, its main character, and some of its verse lines. But while the imitation of sixteenth-century Scottish speech and the pastiche of Lowlands verse may thicken the texture of the dialogue and bring the idiom closer to Shakespeare's, they present the audience with formidable problems:

Crack aff with your great club
The barrel-hoops of love
And let it pour
Like the enchantit quern that boils red-herring broo
Until it gars upswim the goodman's table and his door
While all his house and yard and street
Swill reeken, greasy, het, oer-drownit sax-foot fou—

In his Preface to *Ironhand* (produced 1963), his adaptation of *Goetz von Berlichingen mit der eisernen Hand*, Arden praised the 'vernacular vigour' of Goethe's language. In his own historical play, it is not his aim merely to create or recreate such vigour. He juxtaposes two kinds of speech in order to contrast two modes of life. The virile speech of Armstrong is held up against the etiolated literary language of Sir David Lindsay, which is partly derived by Arden—not without affection and respect but not without parody—from Lindsay's play *Ane Plaesant Satyre on the Thrie Estaitis*. Differentiation of language supports differentiation of character: after his mistress has given herself to the illiterate robber baron, Lindsay's reaction is: 'I wad never claim that I had in ony way foreseen or contrivit this particular development. Gif I had, I wad hae been ane pandar. To the base lusts and deficiencies of humanity.' Though the linguistic scheme may have been conceived with too little consideration for the strain it would impose on the audience, at least Arden's play errs on the side of oversubtlety.

At the end of the Sixties Arden still seemed to be one of

our most promising playwrights. The most traditional, in the sense of being the one most deeply and fruitfully in touch with literary and theatrical tradition, he lacked Pinter's technical expertise and Osborne's quickfire emotionality, but he had a lively mind and a well-developed historical imagination, together with a flair for smelling out the mood of a particular place at a particular time and re-creating the smell with theatrical images. In 1960 he had said: 'What I am deeply concerned with is the problem of translating the concrete life of today into terms of poetry that shall at the one time both illustrate that life and set it within the historical and legendary tradition of our culture.'[15] *Serjeant Musgrave's Dance* had originated from an incident involving British soldiers in Cyprus; *Armstrong's Last Goodnight* was partly inspired by Conor Cruise O'Brien's book on the Congo, *To Katanga and Back*. In both plays Arden was making connections between historical events and contemporary life, and in both plays he fulfilled his intention of writing in 'terms of poetry'. But *Friday's Hiding* (produced 1966), *The Royal Pardon* (produced 1966), *The Hero Rises Up* (produced 1968), *The Ballygombeen Bequest* (produced 1972), *Island of the Mighty* (produced 1972), and *The Non-Stop Connolly Show* (produced 1975), which were all written in collaboration with his wife, Margaretta D'Arcy, were less poetic and more propagandistic.

In comparison with *Serjeant Musgrave's Dance* and *Armstrong's Last Goodnight*, *Island of the Mighty* (the most ambitious and most important of the later plays) is disappointing for its lack of imaginative penetration into its period. There are scattered passages of verse which hark back to the balladlike vigour of the earlier work, as in Gwenhwyvar's post-coital misgivings about the ageing King Arthur:

Observe this disappointed man
Believes himself to be the fresh cold rain
And sunshine that will make the grass grow green.
He stretches out his corded arms and cries:

[15] 'Telling a True Tale', *Encore*, no. 25 (May–June 1960), p. 22.

'Young woman, young woman strip off your clothes
Upon my scaly breast lay down your head.
I am the only champion of God.
Permit yourself to be split in two—'
The sword of Magnus Maximus goes through and through
The blood flows down between the knocking knees
And where it soaks into the ground so dry
The golden corn shall spring up thick and high
The fruits and flowers miraculously arise
All creatures that God made
Into this new-made garden come and feed . . .
So too in the trap-hole of the night *you* cried
You also cried. I was awake. I heard—
The dragon's mouth fell open and there fell out certain words—
Do you remember what they were?

A large proportion of the dialogue is in verse, and poets are prominent in the action, being featured more or less as public-relations officers to the princes, but the bulk of the verse dialogue, like the bulk of the prose, is very thin in texture.

Another writer whose plays are strongly polarized by Shakespeare and the idea of poetic drama is Edward Bond. The question of whether King Lear's consciousness could be translated into the language of Bond might have seemed an unfair question had he not made it unavoidable by writing his own version of Shakespeare's play—*Lear* (produced 1971). He has also written a play about the last years of Shakespeare's life, putting his own attempts at poetic prose into the poet's mouth. In both plays the language is literary and artificial, though Bond had established himself as a playwright by applying his talent for vernacular verismo.

In *The Pope's Wedding* (produced 1962) and *Saved* (produced 1965) his dialogue might seem Pinteresque, but the writing is very much more emotional, even if the emotion is predominantly negative. In Scene 10 of *Saved*, Len is still living in the same house as Pam, who had lost interest in him before she started sleeping with Fred. Fred, the father of her baby, is one of the boys who killed it, but she had little feeling for it, and her feeling for Fred is unaffected.

On the day he is due out of prison she tries to get rid of Len:

PAM: Len. I don't want a keep on at yer. I don't know what's the matter with me. They wan'a put the 'eat on. It's like death. Yer'd get on a lot better with someone else.

LEN: Per'aps 'e ain' comin'.

PAM: They must 'ave all the winders open. It's no life for a fella. Yer ain' a bad sort.

LEN: Yeh. I'm goin' a be late in.

PAM: Don't go.

LEN: You make me money up?

PAM (*after a light pause*): Why can't yer go somewhere?

LEN: Where?

PAM: There's lots a places.

LEN: 'Easy t' say.

PAM: I'll find yer somewhere.

LEN: I ain' scuttlin' off juss t' make room for you t' shag in.

PAM: Yer're a stubborn sod! Don't blame me what 'appens t' yer! Yer ain' messin' me about again.

LEN: I knew that wouldn't last long!

PAM: I'm sick t' death a yer. Clear off!

She goes to the table down left and sits. LEN *goes out left. Pause. He comes back with a cup of tea. He puts it on the table in front of* PAM. *He stands near the table.*

LEN: It'll get cold. (*Pause.*) Did 'e say 'e'd come? (*Pause.*) Did 'e answer any a your letters? (*She reacts.*) I juss wondered!

PAM: I tol' yer before!

LEN: Thass all right then. (*Pause.*)

PAM: It's like winter in 'ere.

The recurrent references to the coldness of the room function quite differently from the inconsequentiality in Pinter. The temperature has its relevance to the emotional temperature of the relationship between Pam and Len, but the main purpose of the sidetracking is to register the strain of carrying on a relationship at all. Len is as stubbornly persistent with her as she is with Fred, and both pursuers and pursued are as grudgingly parsimonious with words as with displays of emotion.

The communication between Pam's parents is still stonier. They don't speak to each other at all until the father has interrupted what might have developed into a sexual relationship between his wife and their lodger:

MARY: Mind out of a drain! I wouldn't let a kid like that touch me if 'e paid for it!

HARRY *comes in. He goes straight to the table.*

HARRY: I don't want to listen.

MARY: Filth!

HARRY: There's bin enough trouble in this 'ouse. Now yer wan'a cause trouble with 'im!

MARY: Don't talk t' me! You!

HARRY (*sees his bread on the floor*): Yer juss wan'a start trouble like there was before! (*He stoops and picks up the bread.*) Middle-age woman—goin' with 'er own daughter's left-overs—'alf 'er age—makin' 'erself a spectacle—look at this! No self-control.

MARY: Filth!

HARRY: Like a child—I pity the lad—must want 'is 'ead tested.

MARY: There'll be some changes in this 'ouse. I ain' puttin' up with this after t'day. Yer can leave my things alone for a start. All this stuff come out a my pocket. I worked for it! I ain' 'avin' you dirtyin' me kitchin. Yer can get yerself some new towels for a start! An' plates! An' knives! An' cups! Yer'll soon find a difference!

HARRY: Don't threaten me—

MARY: An' my cooker! An' my curtains! An' my sheets!

HARRY: Yer'll say somethin' yer'll be sorry for!

In his later, more literary plays Bond's dialogue is much less convincing. *Saved* could have been written only by a moralist, but the moralizing is filtered through the behaviour of inarticulate characters. Bond presents the bare fictional facts without commentary. But in *Lear* the moralizing is articulated directly in the dialogue:

I see. Savages have taken my power. You commit crimes and call them the law! The giant must stand on his toes to prove he's tall!— No, I'm wrong to shout at you, you have so much to do, things to put right, all my mistakes, I understand all that. . . . But he's a little swindler! A petty swindler! Think of the crimes you commit every day in your office, day after day till it's just routine, think of the waste and misery of that! . . . O I know what you think! Whatever's trite and vulgar and hard and shallow and cruel, with no mercy or sympathy—that's what you think, and you're proud of it! You good, decent, honest, upright, lawful men who believe in order—when the last man dies, you will have killed him! I have lived with murderers and thugs, there are limits to their greed and violence, but you decent, honest men devour the earth!

The plainness of the syntax is deliberate, but the monotony and the feebleness of the imagery are not. Even as invective the speech lacks power and impetus, while it is detrimental to provoke comparison, as it does, with the mad speeches on the heath in *King Lear*.

The most ambitious speech in Bond's play comes in the second act, when one of Lear's daughters puts a mirror into his hand:

The king is always on oath! (*He stares down at the mirror.*) No, that's not the king. . . . This is a little cage of bars with an animal in it. (*Peers closer.*) No, no, that's not the king! (*Suddenly gestures violently. The* USHER *takes the mirror.*) Who shut that animal in that cage? Let it out. Have you seen its face behind the bars? There's a poor animal with blood on its head and tears running down its face. Who did that to it? Is it a bird or a horse? It's lying in the dust and its wings are broken. Who broke its wings? Who cut off its hands so that it can't shake the bars? It's pressing its snout on the glass. Who shut that animal in a glass cage? O God, there's no pity in this world. You let it lick the blood from its hair in the corner of a cage with no-where to hide from its tormentors. No shadow, no hole! Let that animal out of its cage! (*He takes the mirror and shows it round.*) Look! Look! Have pity. Look at its claws trying to open the cage. It's drag-ging its broken body over the floor. You are cruel! Cruel! Look at it lying in its corner! It's shocked and cut and shaking and licking the blood on its sides. (USHER *again takes the mirror from* LEAR.) No, no! Where are they taking it now! Not out of my sight! What will they do to it? O God, give it to me! Let me hold it and stroke it and wipe its blood!

Like Archie Rice's speech about being dead behind the eyes, this rhetoric depends for its emotional intensity mainly on the actor's resources. He gets little support from rhythm in the writing, while the texture is thin and the poetic imagery banal. The metaphor of the caged animal is hammered hard without being developed, and a very confused picture emerges from the successive references to wings, hands, snout, hair, and claws. The accusations ('O God, there's no pity in this world' and 'You are cruel! Cruel!') are as tritely declamatory as expostulations in Victorian melo-drama. There is little variation of emotional pressure within the speech, and little shaping. The performer has to make his mind up where the climaxes come, and how to achieve them.

Compared with the use Beckett makes of it in *Endgame*

(written 1955–6, produced 1957), Bond's conception and his realization of *King Lear* are both artless. Beckett's texture, though thin in comparison with Shakespeare's, is immeasurably richer than Bond's:

You weep, and weep, for nothing, so as not to laugh, and little by little . . . you begin to grieve. (*He folds the handkerchief, puts it back in his pocket, raises his head.*) All those I might have helped. (*Pause.*) Helped! (*Pause.*) Saved. (*Pause.*) Saved! (*Pause.*) The place was crawling with them! (*Pause. Violently.*) Use your head, can't you, use your head, you're on earth, there's no cure for that! (*Pause.*) Get out of here and love one another! Lick your neighbour as yourself! (*Pause. Calmer.*) When it wasn't bread they wanted it was crumpets. (*Pause. Violently.*) Out of my sight and back to your petting parties! (*Pause.*) All that, all that! (*Pause.*) Not even a real dog! (*Calmer.*) The end is in the beginning and yet you go on. (*Pause.*) Perhaps I could go on with my story, end it and begin another. (*Pause.*) Perhaps I could throw myself out on the floor. (*He pushes himself painfully off his seat, falls back again.*) Dig my nails into the cracks and drag myself forward with my fingers. (*Pause.*) It will be the end and there I'll be, wondering what can have brought it on and wondering what can have. . . (*he hesitates*) . . . why it was so long coming. (*Pause.*) There I'll be, in the old refuge, alone against the silence and . . . (*he hesitates*) . . . the stillness. If I can hold my peace, and sit quiet, it will be all over with sound, and motion, all over and done with.

It is not only in syntax that Bond's prose is inferior. Beckett's rhythms are richer and livelier. His language is simple, but there is plenty of variation in tone and emotional pressure. Nor is the burden of structuring the speech left to the actor. Beckett has given him a series of difficult transitions, but once he has mastered them, he will have learnt how to shape the speech and how to generate the emotional intensity.

Bond's actor has the apparent advantage of coming to the caged-animal speech after several bouts of harrowingly violent activity, whereas Hamm is confined to his chair throughout the play. The audience might therefore be expected to feel more sympathy with Lear's embittered disenchantment than with Hamm's, but, while neither figure comes to represent suffering humanity as Shakespeare's Lear does, Bond's seems more petulant than Hamm, and self-pitying when he generalizes about pitilessness. Hamm's self-recrimination about 'all those I might have helped' and his contemptuous reference to 'petting parties' do not have as much resonance as King Lear's 'Oh I have ta'en/Too little care of this', and his 'Let copulation thrive', but there is an element of parody in Beckett's paraphrasing. Hamm frequently criticizes and deflates his own pretentiousness with comments like 'All that, all that', and altogether Beckett's borrowing is more suggestively ironic than Bond's. Beckett lets his character share both his awareness of existing at the end of the culture which contains *King Lear*, and his knowledge that he must resort to language which is lyrical or declamatory in an old-fashioned style. But for Hamm, as for Beckett, no other language is available, and the ham actor, however exhausted he is, however long the culture or the play has been running, still has to find his way towards the final climax, even if he'd prefer to lapse into peace and quiet. On one level Hamm represents human consciousness. Inside the brain the show must always go on.

The speech can seem tetchy and maudlin, but only if the actor is unable to understand and exploit the multi-layered comedy which both underlines and undermines the tendency towards melodramatic declamation. Beckett hardly ever fails to expose and ridicule pomposity or phoney emotionality in his speakers, but Bond is humourlessly taken in by his own high seriousness. He felt justified in rewriting *King Lear* because he had convinced himself that he could make it more relevant to the contemporary world. As produced by what Bond calls 'the academic theatre', Shakespeare's play, he says, is 'nice and comfortable. You don't have to question yourself, or change your society. [Lear]'s a Renaissance figure and he doesn't impinge on our society as much as he should. So that I would like to rewrite the play to try and make it more relevant ... to rewrite it so that we now have to use the play for ourselves, for our society, for our time, for our problems.'[16] He tried to streamline and purify the Shake-

---

[16] 'A Discussion with Edward Bond', *Gambit*, no. 17 (1970), p. 24.

spearian text by stripping away heroism, nobility and dignity. It was not his intention to strip away all the poetry, as he has done, but he did intend to refocus the action away from Lear's relationship with the circumambient universe: 'Those three sisters become much more interesting without that old man communing with the heavens and calling down God's judgement.'

Bingo (produced 1973) was still more anti-Shakespearian, focusing on the playwright himself, and depicting him as a 'corrupt seer'. 'His behaviour as a property-owner', Bond says, 'made him closer to Goneril than Lear. He supported and benefited from the Goneril-society—with its prisons, workhouses, whipping, starvation, mutilation, pulpit-hysteria and all the rest of it.' As a landowner at Welcombe, he had, in Bond's terms, to 'side either with the landowners or with the poor who would lose their land and livelihood' if the common fields were enclosed. In fact, Shakespeare seems to have been opposed to the enclosure; but, according to Bond's play, guilt-feelings about social injustice forced him to stop writing and finally to commit suicide. 'My account rather flatters Shakespeare,' Bond insists, in his Introduction to the play (1974). 'If he didn't end in the way shown in the play, then he was a reactionary blimp or some other fool. The only more charitable account is that he was unaware or senile.' (An odd suggestion to make about a man who died at the age of fifty-two.)

Like John Arden, who knew what he wanted to say through Musgrave's mouth before he knew anything else about Musgrave, Bond was subordinating characterization to his didactic starting point. He was under no more obligation to make his portrait of Shakespeare accurate than Shakespeare was with his portrait of Richard III, but in the first half of Bond's play, when Shakespeare says very little, the characterization is much more convincing and compelling than in the second half, when he articulates Bond's ideas in poetic prose of inferior quality:

The last snow this year. Perhaps the last snow I shall see. The last fall. (*He kneels on the ground and picks up the snow.*) How cold. (*He half smiles.*) How perfect, but it only lasts one night. When I was young

I'd have written on it with a stick. A song. The moon over the snow, a woman stares at her dead. . . What? In the morning the sun would melt it into mortality. Writing in the snow—a child's hand fumbling in an old man's beard, and in the morning the old man dies, goes, taking the curls from the child's fingers into the grave, and the child laughs and plays under the dead man's window. New games. Now *I'm* old. Where is the child to touch me and lead me to the grave? Serene. Serene. Is that how they see me? (*He laughs a little.*) I didn't know.
    The dark figures run back across the top of the stage. Their heavy breathing is heard. They go off left.

And later:

I didn't want to die. I could lie in this snow a whole life. I can think now, the thoughts come so easily over the snow and under my shroud. New worlds. Keys turning new locks—pushing the iron open like lion's teeth. Wolves will drag me through the snow. I'll sit in their lair and smile and be rich. In the morning or when I die the sun will rise and melt it all away. The dream. The wolves. The iron teeth. The snow. The wind. My voice. A dream that leads to sleep. (*He sits up.*) I'm dead now. Soon I shall fall down. If I wasn't dead I could kill myself. What is the ice inside me? The plague is hot—this is so cold. The truth means nothing when you hate. Was anything done? Was anything done? I sit in a wound as large as a valley. The sides are smooth and cold and grey. I sit at the bottom and cry at my own death.

As usual in Bond, the sentences are short and the syntax simple, with a great many clauses and phrases joined together by 'and'. In so far as it tries to give an impression of Shakespeare's imagination the soliloquy fails dismally. The mind at work is quite unlike Shakespeare's. The first sentences about snow are badly written, and the first attempt at a poetic image is reminiscent of a twentieth-century imitation of a *haiku*. Though Bond was right to avoid archaic language, he was wrong to put trite metaphors (like 'melt it into mortality') into Shakespeare's mouth. The image about the child's hand in the old man's beard is pointless and laboured, while the yearning for a child to lead him to the grave is sentimental and melodramatic. The metaphor about lion's teeth and locks is confused and confusing, and the suicidal climax imposes an unfair burden on the actor, because the verbal build-up to it gives him virtually no help in reaching the requisite pitch of emotional intensity. Except in the broadest, sketchiest way, the writing does nothing to communicate the quality of the desperation.

Bond's two anti-Shakespearian plays are interesting as key examples of a modish hostility to style, literature, and sophistication. It was, according to Bond, 'Because Jane Austen's imagination was weaker than her knowledge' that 'she could avoid writing about the Napoleonic wars'. It is the writer's duty, he maintains, to gravitate towards deeper involvement in social and political issues: 'Writers who don't develop in this way become shut up in private fantasies, experiments in style, unrewarding obscurities—they become trivial and reactionary.'[17] His view of literature—and of Shakespeare—is at the opposite pole from that of Keats, who appreciated

what quality went to form a Man of Achievement especially in Literature and which Shakespeare possessed so enormously—I mean *Negative Capability*, that is when man is capable of being in uncertainties, Mysteries, doubts, without any irritable reaching after fact and reason.

Tom Stoppard's play *Rosencrantz and Guildenstern Are Dead* (produced 1966; professionally premiered 1967) constitutes as good an example as contemporary drama can provide of Negative Capability. Far from sharing Bond's doctrinaire irritability or his hostility to Shakespeare, to stylishness, and to sophistication, Stoppard makes a virtue out of uncertainty—'Tom Stoppard Doesn't Know' was the title chosen for his 1972 contribution to BBC Television's series 'One Pair of Eyes'. As he has said, the dialogue he wrote for Rosencrantz and Guildenstern was an exteriorization of dialogue he had carried on with himself.[18] Ideologically unpretentious and uncommitted though the play is, its humour, its stylishness, and its sophistication give it a good chance of staying in the repertoire, while it incidentally sketches an answer to the question of why it is inconceivable that a work like *Hamlet* could be written today—an answer based partly on the differences between Shakes-

[17] Introduction to *Bingo* (1974), p. 9.
[18] Interview with Giles Gordon in *The Transatlantic Review* (1968), reprinted in *Behind the Scenes*, ed. Joseph F. McCrindle (1971), p. 81.

pearian verse and modern dramatic dialogue. Stoppard's play is partly about language and style.

After the well-born, well-educated, well-spoken heroes of Noël Coward and Terence Rattigan had become out-moded, and after the first Fifties wave of anti-heroic plays had pushed the iconoclastic working-class lad into the lime-light, it was amusing and refreshing to be offered a neat in-version of a heroic play with the hero relegated to a support-ing role and two attendant lords catapulted into the central position. By putting modern speech-patterns into their mouths and juxtaposing the comic prose scenes with se-quences of Shakespeare's tragedy, Stoppard makes modern clichés appear to be indicative of a cowardice and a slow-wittedness that contrast unfavourably with both Hamlet's courage and Hamlet's language. In the same way that Shake-speare's courtiers fawn on the King, jettisoning honesty and loyalty to their fellow student, the modern phrases seem to play safe, to hold back, to evade the point at issue, while the Elizabethan language takes risks, explores, dis-covers. When Rosencrantz and Guildenstern eavesdrop on Hamlet as he broods about suicide, they appear to be com-mentators from the modern sidelines, taking cowardly refuge in the fumblings and clichés of contemporary speech:

Nevertheless, I suppose one might say that this was a chance. . . . One might well . . . accost him. . . . Yes, it definitely looks like a chance to me. . . . Something on the lines of a direct informal approach . . . man to man . . . straight from the shoulder. . . . Now look here, what's it all about . . . sort of thing. Yes. Yes, this looks like one to be grabbed with both hands, I should say . . . if I were asked. . . . No point in looking at a gift horse till you see the whites of its eyes, etcetera. (*He has moved towards* HAMLET *but his nerve fails. He returns.*) We're overawed, that's our trouble. When it comes to the point we succumb to their personality. . . .

If these are anti-heroes, they have great respect for the heroic mode.

Nor is the play anti-literary. It has roots not only in *Hamlet* and *Waiting for Godot*, but in Eliot's 'The Love Song of J. Alfred Prufrock':

No! I am not Prince Hamlet, nor was meant to be;
Am an attendant lord, one that will do
To swell a progress, start a scene or two

When Edward Albee was asked whether there were elements of Goethe's *Faust* in his 1964 play *Tiny Alice*, he said
'The only way you can avoid having any of these things
creeping in is to be a self-conscious illiterate.'[19] Stoppard
has found a way of leaning lightly on the shoulders of
writers from whom he borrows heavily, and this is preferable
to punching them in the stomach, as Bond does. At the
end of *Jumpers* (produced 1972) Stoppard parodied James
Joyce; in *Travesties* (produced 1974) Joyce was introduced
as a character, with Oscar Wilde as the main object of
parody. Joyce himself had made parody one of the archi-
tectural principles of *Ulysses*, and to the extent that modern
literature is dependent on previous literature, it can only
gain by bringing the dependence into comic focus. But for
the contemporary dramatist, the question of literary allusions is often complicated by political considerations.
The idea of a working-class audience is no longer mythical,
and the public that most young playwrights are aiming at
is not highly literate. Between the two extreme positions
represented by Stoppard and Bond (parody and anti-
literature) there is a whole spectrum of possibilities, involving varying degrees of self-consciousness about literature and
language. It is dangerous to cultivate indifference to style:
the consequences of unselfconsciousness in writing can be
even worse than the consequences of self-consciousness.
But fashion has swung against the literary tradition, and
many playwrights want to dissociate themselves from it.
Stoppard is exceptional, and so is Charles Wood, who sculpts
his prose as carefully as if it were verse.[20] Sometimes he
even prints it like verse. This is done not to get away from
the speech-patterns of colloquial English, but to pin them
down more precisely on the page. Dealing with uneducated
characters, Wood has not laid the dialogue out as verse, but,

[19] Interview with Michael Nardacci and Walter Chura in *Beverwyck* (1965),
reprinted in *The Playwrights Speak*, ed. Walter Wager (1969), p. 36.
[20] See below, pp. 64–8.

like Pinter, he has written dialogue stylishly and rhythmic-
ally. The younger generation of playwrights is tending to
veer away from both style and rhythm.

Barrie Keeffe is an example. In *Gimme Shelter*, a trilogy
of one-act plays produced between 1975 and 1977, he
emerged as a sturdy champion of the semi-literate. One of
the plays, *Gotcha*, centres on a boy leaving a comprehensive
school and, justifiably, boiling over with indignation at the
ineffectuality and indifference of the people who have been
responsible for educating him. They have not paid sufficient attention to him. The headmaster does not even
know his name.

Comprehensive! (*He spits.*) Me brother, me brother wow, what he said
about it when I come here! Chance for you, kiddo, he said to me.
Secondary school he went to. No hope. Chucked in there. Factory
fodder, but this comprehensive! Paradise. So different he said . . . and
he supposed to know. Knows the mayor, delivered his leaflets for
him at elections, me brother did. Knew all about what was gonna
happen in this new school. This is your big chance, kiddo, he says. . .
(*Pause.*) Got it wrong. Just the same. Only bigger. Anything you want
here, they said. Yeah. If you're clever, if you're bright, big hope . . .
glittering prizes! Just the same, as it was for me brother . . . just . . .
the same. Only bigger. Achievement . . . successes . . . only way it's
judged . . . all them O levels, all them A levels, all them clever bastards
going to university. What a clever headmaster, what a smashing lot a
teachers, what a great school. What a fantastic school—What about us?
Who don't do O levels? What about me, eh? How good is this? (*He
throws the report on the floor. Stamps on it. Stands breathing
deeply.*)
    HEAD: It is . . . never easy to build a perfect world . . . a new
Jerusalem on Canning Town marshland. . . . It's a gradual process,
slow steps . . . making a net of tighter mesh . . . it takes time.

Barrie Keeffe could not be accused, as Eliot and Pinter
could, of treating uneducated speech with critical conde-
scension. The evasive clichés and the tired cultural
allusions in the language of the headmaster help to ensure
that he will get less sympathy from the audience than the
boy will. The speech of the other teachers is equally flabby,
but theatrically there is little vigour or vitality in the boy's
language either, while its lifelessness is valuable only in so
far as it helps to show him as the victim of a system that

has not taught him how to communicate. In the third play, *Getaway*, when Keeffe tries to penetrate into the inner life of his anonymous character, the exploration of sensitivity misfires. After threatening three of the teachers that he would cause an explosion by dropping a cigarette into the petrol tank of a motor cycle, the Kid has been sent to a Borstal:

I had nightmares in Feltham . . . that I'd dropped the fag, the petrol tank went . . . the bodies burned . . . the eyes popped and the stomachs exploded and. . .the cinders stuck all over my face, burned flesh, like sticky burnt plastic . . . couldn't peel it off . . . it closed my eyes . . . I couldn't see . . . Couldn't see that that was worth it.

This is no more like the language of Hemingway's 'The Killers' than the boy's sensitivity is like that of Raskolnikov, but it poses the problem that Steiner formulated. The language is inadequate to the consciousness, and however successful the trilogy is in making us sympathize with the Kid, his inarticulacy sets unavoidable limits on the extent to which he can interest or involve us.

In Genet's 1959 play *Les Nègres* the black characters want to reject white civilization totally. But, to be complete, repudiation of the culture must include renunciation of the language. One character who talks about his father is reprimanded for letting tenderness creep into his voice when the situation of his people requires only hatred; he is told to invent 'if not words then phrases which cut instead of joining'. Left alone together, two black lovers have great difficulty in expressing themselves without using the vocabulary of the whites. The radical playwright is in a comparable position. Hostility to the dominant society and the dominant culture enforces hostility to the literary tradition and to current standards of good writing. He may feel morally obliged to write badly.

2 Innovation and conservatism

All the most important innovations in postwar European drama have been made by writers with strong feelings about language and the theatre. In 1937 Beckett was proposing a 'literature of the un-word',[1] and *En attendant Godot*, written in 1948 when he was forty-two, could have been conceived only by someone with a strong aversion to the theatrical *status quo*. The script for his 1947 play *Eleuthéria*, which has never been produced or published, contains instructions for an actor planted in the auditorium to storm up on the stage protesting that 'It's like watching a game of chess between two tenth-rate players', and that he is 'nauseated, bored to extinction, worn out, flabbergasted by such stupidity'. From *Godot* to *That Time* (1974) and *Footfalls* (1975) Beckett has explored and exploited the medium by rejecting the resources it puts at his disposal, austerely using less scenery, less movement, less visual variation, less lighting changes, less of the actors' personalities and even less of their bodies, submerging them in dustbins, urns, or sand, and, in *Not I* (1973), concealing everything but the actress's mouth.

Ionesco was thirty-six in 1948 when he wrote his first play, *La Cantatrice chauve* (*The Bald Soprano*), without any thought of having it performed, as it was in 1950. He had consistently disliked both plays and actors for twenty years. Later he designated *La Cantatrice chauve* as an 'anti-play'. 'It was only a parody of a play, a comedy of comedies.' Though, since childhood, he had loved Punch-and-Judy shows, he had been worried by the physical presence of actors on the stage. 'Every gesture, every atti-

---

[1] Letter to Axel Kaun, cited by Laurence E. Harvey in *Samuel Beckett: Poet and Critic* (1970), pp. 433–4.

tude, every speech spoken on the stage destroyed for me a world that these same gestures, attitudes and speeches were specifically designed to evoke; destroyed it even before it could be created.'[2]

What Genet disliked most about the theatre was its frivolity: 'Its *raison d'être* is exhibitionism.'[3] Writing *Les Bonnes* (1947) he was hoping

> to achieve the abolition of characters— which usually stand up only by psychological convention—in favour of signs as remote as possible from what they should at first signify, but in touch with it none the less, in order to link the author to the audience by this one means. . . . The highest modern drama has been expressed every day for two thousand years in the sacrifice of the mass. . . . Theatrically I know nothing more effective than the elevation of the host.[4]

His other model for what theatre ought to be was in the improvisation that occurred unselfconsciously in children's games.

Peter Handke is more violently anti-theatrical. No play has ever depended less on character or on plot than *Publikumsbeschimpfung* (*Insulting the Audience*, written 1965) or has ever approximated more closely to the condition of nonrepresentational art. Like Wittgenstein, Handke is constantly concerned about the non-relationship between objects and words. He told an interviewer that his play *Kaspar* (produced 1968) 'consists primarily of sentence games and sentence models dealing with the impossibility of *expressing* anything in language. . . . I think a sentence doesn't mean something else: it means itself.'[5]

No contemporary English playwright seems so concerned about language or so hostile to the existing theatre as these four. Without having been so radical or so consistent in their experimentation, English playwrights have not been immune to the influence of the European innovators. Pinter's first three plays, *The Room*,[6] *The Birthday Party*

[2] *Notes and Counter-Notes*, trans. Donald Watson (1974), pp. 15, 189.
[3] Letter to J. -J. Pauvert, printed as the Preface to *Les Bonnes* (1954).
[4] ibid.
[5] Interview with Artur Joseph, trans. E. B. Ashton, *The Drama Review*, vol. XV, no. 1 (Fall 1970).
[6] See above, pp. 8–9.

(written 1957, produced 1958), and *The Dumb Waiter* (written 1957; produced in Germany 1959, in England 1960)—are strikingly insistent in their refusal to define or specify. Beckett's characters are unable to provide each other with information about their present situation or about their recent experience or about current events in the world outside; Pinter's tend to be more perverse, confusing and disturbing the audience as they confuse and disturb each other, misleading each other in order to provoke. Pinter constantly violates the theatrical convention which makes us assume that characters are telling the truth unless clear indications are given that they are not. His characters are forgetful or dishonest about the past, vague or secretive about their intentions, ignorant or biased about their motivations. Their behaviour is liable to be inconsistent both with their explanations of it and in itself. But whereas Beckett's settings are never naturalistic or specific about place and time, Pinter uses realistic sets, planting his characters firmly in a recognizable social context.

The most experimental phase in his development seems to have been inspired by Beckett's 1964 play *Play*, which immobilized its three characters in urns, relegating their triangular relationship to the past. All they do is talk about it—not to each other—from a Limbo present. Pinter's *Landscape* (broadcast 1968, staged 1969) and *Silence* (staged with it in a double bill) also immobilize the actors and relegate most of the action to the past. Like Beckett, Pinter was repudiating the resources the medium put at his disposal, approximating to the condition of radio drama. (Though *Landscape* was broadcast before being staged, it was written for the theatre.) In *Landscape* the two characters are sitting in the kitchen of a country house, but the text consists not so much of dialogue as of two interwoven monologues. The speakers are both more alive than the three characters in *Play*—they have a present and a future as well as a past; they have desires, needs, moods—but the action consists entirely of words and sounds. While *Landscape* has no movement in it, *Silence* has very little, and the characters are less often talking to each other than to themselves about themselves. The relationships they have had are not dramatized but evoked by the words, as are the locales. The stage setting provides only a generalized background. The play is like a dramatic poem, spoken by three voices. The inter-relationship of their styles is clearer and more important than the personal inter-relationship.

Without having written *Landscape* and *Silence*, Pinter could not have written *Old Times* (produced 1971) which neither immobilizes nor insulates its characters but explores new kinds of fluidity in and between them, finding new ways of circumventing the tiresome business of opening doors and coming in and going out. At the beginning of the action Anna, who is more dimly lit than Kate and Deeley, is neither wholly present nor wholly absent, and when she comes downstage into the brighter light, it is clear that the movement does not signify an entrance. She has heard part of their conversation. There are also casual shifts in time, forward into the period immediately after dinner, and twenty years backward to the time when Kate and Anna were both secretaries, sharing a flat. Sometimes re-enactment of the past alternates with reminiscence, sometimes the past and the present are fused, stage action corresponding approximately to action inside the mind of one or another of the characters. Identity becomes volatile as Deeley's memories of the girls seem to merge. Sometimes the two of them appear almost interchangeable. The critics disagreed about whether Anna was 'actually' present in the room or just a presence in the memories of the other two. But a playwright is entitled to oscillate between two such alternatives or even have it both ways at the same time.

In *No Man's Land* (produced 1975) the discrepancies go still further: there are contradictory indications about whether the two men have met before. At first it looks as though they haven't; later Hirst is claiming to have seduced Spooner's wife. There is also a sharper discontinuity between the sequences. Hirst, a rich man of letters ensconced in a Hampstead mansion, and Spooner, a penurious poet, play a series of variations in the roles of host and guest, house-owner and visitor at pains not to outstay his welcome, or at least not to appear to. In one sequence Hirst seems not even to recognize the man we have seen him entertaining, and in another he greets him like an equal who has only just arrived: 'Charles, how nice of you to drop in.'

As pieces of narrative, these two full-length plays are less straightforward than Pinter's first three full-length plays, *The Birthday Party*, *The Caretaker* (produced 1960), and *The Homecoming* (produced 1965), which never move backward in time. But neither *Old Times* nor *No Man's Land* is experimental in the same sense that *Landscape* and *Silence* are. Whereas the two one-act plays honestly fulfil the tasks they set themselves, completely realizing their potential, there is an air of compromise about both the full-length plays, which might both have been better if (like Beckett's later work) they had been written without any concern for filling an evening in the theatre. Stylish and intriguing though they both are, they tend to repeat themselves and to repeat tricks Pinter has played before. The explorer is slowing his pace to that of the entertainer.

At the most formative stage of John Osborne's development he was probably being impeded by the proscenium at the Royal Court Theatre. From 1956 to 1972, virtually all his plays were staged there, and from *The Entertainer* (1957) onwards he was writing with the Royal Court stage and auditorium in mind. *The Entertainer* and *Luther* (produced 1961) were written when he was under the influence of Brecht, who had used such devices as the alienation effect mainly to destroy the illusion of the fourth wall (see p. 133), drawing attention to the play as an artefact.

Samuel Beckett and Bertolt Brecht have little in common, but they both knew that tragedy could be mated with broad farce to produce healthy bastard progeny. *Waiting for Godot*, which had its English premiere in 1955, drew on both music hall and the comedy routines of such film comedians as Buster Keaton and Charlie Chaplin. Brecht found precedent in both Elizabethan drama and in vaudeville for violating the convention that actors must never signal their awareness of the audience's presence, and his language was influenced both by the poetry of the Elizabethans and by the vernacular directness of vaudeville. Osborne is neither a poet nor able to tap the vitality of colloquial speech, but in *The Entertainer* he followed Brecht through the hole in the invisible fourth wall. The scenes that present Archie as a stand-up comedian force the audience to play a collective role as the audience in the variety theatre, while the decaying art form and the crumbling variety theatre are implicitly equated with the cultural and political situation of Britain. The play owes much of its resonance to this equation.

In *Luther* the auditorium becomes a marketplace when Tetzel tries to sell Indulgences, and the audience becomes a congregation when Luther preaches from the steps of the Castle Church at Wittenberg. But the later plays—*Time Present* (produced 1968), *Hotel in Amsterdam* (produced 1968), and *West of Suez* (produced 1971)—fall back behind an invisible fourth wall. As Osborne threw off the Brechtian influence he instinctively retreated towards the structure of the well-made play. His 1972 play *A Sense of Detachment* faces up to the fact that it consists of a performance inside a theatre. It is his most unrealistic play and the only one that doesn't tell a story. Formally it is his most original, though it owes quite a lot to Handke's *Publikumsbeschimpfung*. The actors on stage present themselves as actors, while two actors in the auditorium pose as spectators—a beer-swilling football fan in a box and a disapproving Tory who moves about between the stalls and the circle. Most of the play's dynamic depends on insult and interruption, and Osborne's intention is that the two actors planted in the auditorium should help to provoke the rest of the audience into contributing some insults and interruptions. The momentum runs out long before the end, as the tension comes more and more to depend on a collage of quotations in contrasting styles, Elizabethan love lyrics being juxtaposed with excerpts from a pornographic catalogue of picture books and films. The dialogue also incorporates speeches on a random selection of subjects including the

Irish situation, women, and the early sexual experiences of a character with at least some biographical affinities to John Osborne.

Osborne's earlier play *Inadmissible Evidence* (1964) is better than anything he has written since. Though it does not try to break out of the proscenium convention, it does incorporate several stylistic experiments. It opens with a dream sequence which is almost expressionistic, but it reverts to naturalism for a long scene set in a solicitor's office. We are over halfway through the play before we find that the action is again being filtered to us through the consciousness of the solicitor, Bill Maitland, who is becoming incapable of focusing clearly on external reality. Three divorce clients are played by the same actress—a device which helps us inside Maitland's muddled mind by suggesting that it can no longer differentiate between them. In the first of the three sequences we see that he can't concentrate on what the woman is saying about her husband without being paralysingly reminded of himself. Everyone, she says, is drawing away from him. Even the children hardly notice him, and though she hates to see him rejected and scorned, she has to leave him. Talking to the second client, Bill again identifies with the unseen husband as she reads from the divorce petition. He quotes from the man's replies, the dialogue being contrived so that each point is answered as soon as it is made, while each answer seems to be applying both to Mr. Tonks and to Bill himself:

MRS. TONKS: That the respondent refused to cease from having intercourse during the time of the petitioner's menstrual periods at 42 Macwilliam Street and number 11 Wicker Street, notwithstanding the petitioner's entreaties. . . .

BILL: There were difficulties between us. Such that my wife failed to reach satisfaction.

MRS. TONKS: That. On frequent occasions at the said addresses whilst he was having intercourse with petitioner he did. . . .

BILL: My wife visited the Marriage Guidance Council on at least three occasions who told her they believed the difficulty was due to my wife's reluctance. . . .

MRS. TONKS: Notwithstanding the fact that he knew the petitioner found this conduct revolting and upsetting.

The three sequences are progressively less realistic. The dialogue with the third client is like a game of free association:

> MRS. ANDERSON: He was able to be at home most of the time, but when he was away, never more than for the odd day or two, he would accuse me of going out with men.
> BILL: Well. She thinks I've got mistresses all over London. They both do. And it's not even true. Worse luck. No, thank God.
> MRS. ANDERSON: He said I ought to go on the streets.
> BILL: You might have met me then. You might have been worse off.
> MRS. ANDERSON: I have never been with anyone apart from my husband.

Like Pinter in *Landscape* and *Silence*, Osborne is substituting interwoven monologues for dialogue, a technique he might have been able to develop if he had persevered. But with all the experiments in stylization that he makes in *Inadmissible Evidence*, he seems more interested in gaining a foothold than in using it to move forward. He is technically promiscuous. Once having found a solution to a problem, he drops it, never using it to solve another.

There's a stage direction in the printed script which says that in some of the long telephone conversations, the audience should sometimes be in doubt about whether or not there is anyone at the other end of the line. This is a device which can work extremely well, temporarily solving the problem that had bedevilled both *Look Back in Anger* and *The Entertainer*. Osborne's chief talent is for writing monologue, and though Billy and Phoebe in *The Entertainer* are given better speeches than any of the supporting characters in *Look Back in Anger*, there is little real give-and-take in the conversation. The principal innovations of *Inadmissible Evidence* are techniques for spotlighting isolation. In the sequences with the divorce clients the lack of give-and-take constitutes the theatrical point; in the telephone conversations, Bill's solipsism is focused, and, as in the sequences where Archie is functioning as a stand-up comedian, there is no need for an onstage audience which will contribute perfunctory interruptions to the central monologue. Not realizing the value of his discovery, Osborne embarrassingly reinstates the onstage audience in Bill's scene with his daughter, which introduces yet another form of stylization, by making the girl unrealistically silent. The unfortunate actress has to move about the stage, letting herself be admonished, admired, and hugged, without uttering a syllable. In so far as the character exists, it is not so much an individual daughter as an Aunt Sally representative of the younger generation for Bill to measure himself against:

You are unself-conscious, which I am not. You are without guilt, which I am not. Quite rightly. Of course, you are stuffed full of paltry relief for emergent countries, and marches and boycotts and rallies, you, you kink your innocent way along tirelessly to all that poetry and endless jazz and folk worship, and looking gay and touching and stylish all at the same time. But there isn't much loving in any of your kindnesses, Jane, not much kindness, not even cruelty, really, in any of you, not much craving for the harm of others, perhaps just a very easy, controlled, sharp, I mean 'sharp' pleasure in discomfiture.

Osborne's over-tolerance towards stylistic discontinuity in his plays and the once-is-enough profligacy of the stylistic experiments he makes in *Inadmissible Evidence* both derive from a lack of interest in style. The character of Bill could never have become so vivid, or the play so resonant, without its stylistic innovations, but Osborne's later work, which lapses back formally into conservatism, suggests that he is unaware of this.

Joe Orton's importance as an innovator was proportional to his influence in reinstating farce as a vehicle for subject matter not normally accommodated by it. Joan Littlewood had taken the first step with her influential production of *Oh What a Lovely War* (1963), which transformed the First World War into a pierrot show, recreating the horrors of trench warfare alongside comedy which provoked healthy laughter at the human absurdities of the situation and at the inhumane absurdity of those who were leading men into it. Songs of the period, full of patriotic nostalgia, were counterpointed against casualty statistics, facts flickering across an electrified ribbon screen. Dialogue was reduced to disconnected nonsense, whether it was the gibberish spoken by soldiers during bayonet practice or the laconic conversation, as international tycoons shot at wildfowl, about using neutral trade routes for exporting arms to the enemy. Orton, whose first play, *The Ruffian on the Stair*, was broadcast in 1964, was the first to follow the cue for the theatrical exploitation of the sick joke; Charles Wood and Peter Nichols were next, Wood applying it to military subject matter in most of his plays, Nichols applying it to a spastic child in *A Day in the Death of Joe Egg* (1967) and to the army in *Privates on Parade* (1977).

Orton's *Entertaining Mr. Sloane* (produced 1964) sets up a comic contrast between the invulnerable calmness of the pseudo-genteel characters and their violent sexual and criminal behaviour. Their speech is quaint, comic and convincing, imbued with an affected literariness which can be based only on very careful observation of colloquial habits:

KATH: That seat is erected to the memory of Mrs. Gwen Lewis. She was a lady who took a lot of trouble with invalids. (*Pause.*) It was near that seat that my baby was thought of.

SLOANE: On that seat?

KATH (*shyly*): Not on it exactly. Near by. . . .

SLOANE: In the bushes? . . . (*She giggles.*)

KATH: Yes. (*Pause.*) He was rough with me.

SLOANE: Uncomfortable, eh?

KATH: I couldn't describe my feelings. (*Pause.*) I don't think the fastening of this thing I'm wearing will last much longer. (*The snapshots slip from her hand.*) There! you've knocked the photos on the floor. (*Pause: he attempts to move; she is almost on top of him.*) Mr. Sloane. . . (*Rolls on to him.*) You should wear more clothes, Mr. Sloane. I believe you're as naked as me. And there's no excuse for it. (*Silence.*) I'll be your mamma. I need to be loved. Gently. Oh! I shall be so ashamed in the morning. (*Switches off the light.*) What a big heavy baby you are. Such a big heavy baby.

The central joke is that the murderer becomes the victim: having killed their Dadda, Sloane cannot protest when Kath and Ed make a deal to share his sexual favours.

Loot (1966) is both funnier and more committed. It pushes into taboo areas, poking fun at the religiose reverence which surrounds death, and it plays on the insecurities of the audience by showing that by investing trust in policemen and nurses we are giving them *carte blanche* for criminal or even murderous behaviour. At the same time, by combining breakneck speed with languid non-involvement, the play persuades us to accept details that might have been highly offensive. An embalmed corpse is taken out of its coffin and humped about the stage, while the vital organs are being kept in a small casket in the hall. A glass eye gets lost and is found by a bewildered detective; the false teeth are brandished and clicked like castanets. Orton opened a most unlikely vein for comedy and exploited it hilariously. The dialogue is more stylized than in *Entertaining Mr. Sloane*, but the texture is rich, and the detail dense. The nurse makes no secret of her designs on the widower:

> FAY: The funeral will occupy you for an hour or so. Afterwards a stroll to the house of a man of God, a few words of wisdom and a glance through the Catholic Truth Society's most recent publication should set your adrenalin flowing. Then a rest. I don't want you overstrained.
>
> McLEAVY: When did you say you were leaving? I don't wish to cause you any inconvenience.
>
> FAY: I'll decide when you've inconvenienced me long enough.
>
> McLEAVY: You're very good to me.
>
> FAY: As long as you appreciate my desire to help. My own life has been unhappy. I want yours to be different.
>
> McLEAVY: You've had an unhappy life?
>
> FAY: Yes. My husbands died. I've had seven altogether. One a year on average since I was sixteen. I'm extravagant you see. And then I lived under stress near Penzance for some time. I've had trouble with institutions. Lack of funds. A court case with my hairdresser. I've been reduced to asking people for money before now.
>
> McLEAVY: Did they give it to you?
>
> FAY: Not willingly. They had to be persuaded. (*With a bright smile.*) I shall accompany you to your lawyers. After the reading of your wife's will you may need skilled medical assistance.
>
> McLEAVY (*with a laugh*): I don't think there are any surprises in store. After a few minor bequests the bulk of Mrs. McLeavy's fortune comes to me.
>
> FAY: I've also arranged for your doctor to be at your side. You've a weak heart.

What the Butler Saw (produced 1969) was less successful. If comedy, as James Agate maintained, is about unreal characters in real situations, and farce about real characters in unreal situations, *What the Butler Saw* is too patently about unreal characters in unreal situations. It tries to repeat the trick of making the audience feel insecure when figures of authority are shown to be unreliable: an irresponsible doctor and a crazy psychiatrist are eager to certify a sane patient. But the confusions of identity and the pretexts for undressing the characters seem mechanical, while the dialogue sometimes proceeds as a random series of jokes:

> MRS. PRENTICE: Whose fault is it if our marriage is on the rocks? You're selfish and inconsiderate. Don't push me too far. (*With a toss of her head.*) I might sleep with someone else.
> PRENTICE: Who?
> MRS. PRENTICE: An Indian student.
> PRENTICE: You don't know any.
> MRS. PRENTICE: New Delhi is full of them.
> PRENTICE (*staring, aghast*): You can't take lovers in Asia! The air fare would be crippling.
>
> MRS. PRENTICE *drops ice into her glass and ignores* DR. PRENTICE, *her nose in the air.* DR. PRENTICE *stands beside her and shouts into her ear.*
>
> Your irresponsible behaviour causes me untold anxiety. A man exposed himself to you last summer.
> MRS. PRENTICE (*without looking at him*): I didn't see anything.
> PRENTICE: And your disappointment marred our holiday.

As a man, Orton had an uncanny flair for steering his life into situations which can be described only as farcical. He was extraordinarily attractive to incongruities. How many other people ever find themselves watching television in the presence of a corpse? In his diaries he wrote extremely well about such incidents, but it was only in *Loot* that he managed, as a playwright, to blend the outrageous with the real.

Tom Stoppard has proved to be more of an innovator in his radio plays and his one-act plays for the stage than in his full-length plays. Like Pinter, he owes a lot to Beckett. As he has said, *Godot* 'redefined the minima of theatrical validity'; *Rosencrantz and Guildenstern Are Dead* followed it in centring on the inactivity enforced by waiting, and in dispensing with the kind of plot that is engineered to arouse and sustain an audience's curiosity about what is going to happen next. But whereas Beckett's originality as a dramatist depends partly on his anti-theatrical instincts and partly on his ability to mint a vocabulary of theatrical images to express his poetic vision, Stoppard is less of a poet and less immune to the appeal of spectacular visual effects. Nor can it be said that a personal vision is being articulated in such images as the pyramid of acrobats in *Jumpers*, or the posturing in elegant costumes which produces the most memorable pictorial effects in *Travesties*. Stoppard is less *Angst*-ridden than Beckett, and more content to take his bearings from existing cultural maps.

His radio plays are extraordinarily inventive. *If You're Glad I'll Be Frank* (broadcast 1966) is about a woman who provides a voice for the Post Office's speaking clock and about a bus driver who is liable to dismount from a crowded bus in order to telephone her from a public callbox. In *Albert's Bridge* (broadcast 1967) a boy works as a bridge-painter because he is happy only when alone, high above the chaotic bustle of the big city, seeing it on a scale which makes it look orderly. Ingeniously constructed in a complex pattern of flashbacks, *Artist Descending a Staircase* (broadcast 1972) is slung between two ambiguities. One is a tape-recorded sound which might be either a man snoring or a fly buzzing; the other is an image in the memory of a beautiful blind girl who started a love affair with the wrong man because of a confusion that occurred when she was losing her sight.

The 1970 stage play *After Magritte* opens with a tableau suggestive of a modernist painting: an old lady lying on an ironing board, a half-naked man wearing thigh-length green rubber fishing waders, a kneeling woman in a ball gown, a lampshade on a pulley counterweighted by a basket overflowing with fruit, furniture stacked against the street door. The dialogue proceeds very funnily to provide explanations for everything we have seen, and the action culminates in a tableau which is equally grotesque. The principle behind *Dogg's Our Pet* (produced 1971) is both Magrittean and Wittgensteinian. The dialogue is constructed from a vocabulary of no more than about fifty words, all based on certain sound values, and nearly all given several meanings, some of which are quite unrelated to their normal meanings. 'Plank', for instance, means 'here', and 'block' means 'next'.

But apart from *Dirty Linen* and *New-Found-Land* (produced 1976), which are both lightweight and less experimental, Stoppard has not produced any one-act plays since *Dogg's Our Pet*, and though his full-length plays contain surrealistic sequences, like the nightmare that ends *Jumpers*, he does not seem to be committing his imagination to experiments that challenge the limitations of the medium. There are amusing stylistic tricks, like the passage at the beginning of *Travesties* in which no normal English is spoken for several minutes, and the almost incomprehensible Joycean speech at the end of *Jumpers*:

Indeed, if moon mad herd instinct, is God dad the inference?—to take another point: If goons in mood, by Gad is sin different or banned good, f'r'instance?—thirdly: out of the ether, random nucleic acid testes or neither universa vice, to name but one—fourthly: If the necessary being isn't, surely mother of invention as Voltaire said, not to mention Darwin different from the origin of the specious—to sum up: Super, both natural and stitious, sexual ergo cogito er go-go sometimes, as Descartes said, and who are we?

But these are *jeux d'esprit*, not experiments, and there are no visual effects or stage pictures as original as the best in his one-act plays.

Without having much interest either in style or in challenging the limitations of the medium, Arnold Wesker has been important as a theatrical reformer. Working-class themes and working-class characters had not been totally excluded from the English stage before 1955, but D. H. Lawrence's plays had made no impression on the theatre of the Twenties, and not even Lawrence had ever cut such large slices of working life and bundled them so unceremoniously on to a stage as Wesker did, saying, in effect: 'See how little I have to transcribe in order to give you drama.' Nor, in 1955, would anyone have thought it possible to make a large-scale success out of a one-act play with 29 characters and with the whole action set in a kitchen. No one else would have believed that a trilogy of plays about Jewish Communists and Norfolk farm labourers would stand any chance of being produced. And no one could have guessed that the West End would welcome an all-male play which seems to be about national service, but grows into a swingeing attack on our social system. It ends with the national anthem played to a seated audience.

Admittedly *The Kitchen*, which was staged in 1959, had been written in 1956 for television, and it was the idea of John Dexter, the director, to structure the stage version with a slow, quiet, dreamy interlude between the two episodes of bustling movement. Wesker had provided a script in which actions produce the main effects—the actions of cooks and waitresses doing their work, a dance, an accident, a practical joke, a quarrel, a cook running berserk. Like Arthur Miller in *A Memory of Two Mondays* (produced 1955), Wesker shows how the rhythm of a working routine can determine not only the rhythm of the relationships that are possible inside it but the rhythm of the characters' lives. It is not just that everything else they do has to be fitted around their work: they are what they are because of their work and they express themselves most directly in the way they work. Dexter's decision to eliminate food had the effect of sharpening the focus on the cooks' miming movements, and they characterized themselves all the more clearly through the way they dished out non-existent fish or rolled out imaginary pastry. At the same time, the style of the production made this naturalistic play look experimental.

The chief source of unevenness in Wesker's plays is the separation between action and argument. His object was not merely to tell stories but to break down 'the facile blind arguments, the platitudinous phrases which are the barricades of the man in the street to anything new'. He wanted to 'give people an insight to an aspect of life which they may not have had before; and further, I want to impart to them some of the enthusiasm I have for that life. I want to teach.'[7] *Roots* (produced 1959) was slow-moving but powerful in its attack on the tendency of pop culture to brutalize the working classes. It succeeds better than the other two plays in the trilogy, *Chicken Soup with Barley* (produced 1958) and *I'm Talking about Jerusalem* (produced 1960), because Ronnie, the main mouthpiece for Wesker's arguments, is kept offstage. We hear his opinions at second hand, through the mouth of his girlfriend, a farm labourer's daughter. The cultural life of her family is measured against what she has learnt from Ronnie: Mendelssohn and Bizet versus pop songs, books versus comics, art versus entertainment, discussion versus chatter, mental activity versus mental stagnation. The conflict between the two ways of life surfaces most often in arguments between Beatie and her family, but the best moments of the play occur when Beatie's proselytizing energy surges into action, as when she makes her sister Jenny tidy up her house, dragging a muddled miscellany of clothes from a cupboard to fold them up, or when she tries to make her mother listen to Bizet and breaks into an exuberant dance, clapping her hands to the rhythm until her mother joins in. But it is only at the end of the play that argument and action are triumphantly welded together as Beatie, who has been jilted by Ronnie, finds out by talking that she is no longer parroting his opinions. She has made them into her own.

Chips with Everything (produced 1962) is concerned, like *The Kitchen*, not with a family but with a large group of characters assembled in a working situation. In the later play Wesker is more adroit at translating his argument against pop culture into stage action. When the patronizing Wing Commander tries to get the airmen to sing pop songs, Pip persuades one boy to recite a seventeenth-century dirge and the others to sing an old peasant revolt song. The meticulous stage directions for the coke-stealing sequence show how much Wesker had learnt from Dexter's direction of *The Kitchen*:

[7] 'Let Battle Commence', *Encore*, vol. V, no. 5 (November–December 1958), p. 19.

GINGER *dashes to wire, and places chair—dashes to other side of stage.* PIP *runs to chair, jumps up and over,* DODGER *runs to take chair away and joins* GINGER. *The* GUARD *appears and carries on round.* DODGER *runs back, places chair.* WILFE *runs to chair with another, jumps on it, and drops chair into* PIP's *hands, runs off.* DODGER *runs on, and withdraws chair. The* GUARD *appears, and continues.* DODGER *runs on with chair again.* ANDREW *runs with buckets to chair, jumps up and passes them to* PIP. GINGER *runs to take chair away.* GUARD *appears, and continues. In like process, two buckets are returned 'full' of Coke.*

And generally the dialogue is more economical and more incisive. For some of it Wesker refines the alloy of Air Force slang: 'But I will tear and mercilessly scratch the scorching daylights out of anyone who smarts the alec with me—and we've got some 'ere. I can see them, you can tell them.'

Wesker's most experimental play, *The Four Seasons* (produced 1965), was one of his least successful. The relationship between the lovers progresses seasonally, budding, ripening, and going to seed during the year they spend together. It is the least political of Wesker's plays and the least conventionally plotted. We never find out who the house belongs to, or why it is left empty for a year, or how Adam and Beatrice manage about food and electricity and water supply. Or how they met and became involved. Suspense is sustained throughout the first of the four sequences by the expedient of keeping Beatrice silent. She reacts wordlessly to all Adam's efforts to draw her into conversation. (Bergman's film *The Silence* was first shown at the end of 1963; *The Four Seasons* was written between May 1964 and September 1965.) But the play deteriorates when they start talking to each other. No play of Wesker's has depended more on dialogue, and it is not redeemed from wordiness and facile lyricism by the rare sequences of action, such as the singing lesson and the sequence in which they relate to each other through cooking an apple strudel.

Just as Stoppard could not have written *Rosencrantz and Guildenstern Are Dead* without the example of Beckett,

Edward Bond could not have written any of his more mature plays without the example of Brecht, though the superficial evidence of influence is less important than the deep infiltration. Bond's first two plays, *The Pope's Wedding* and *Saved*, cannot be called Brechtian, and that *Early Morning* (produced 1968) can is apparent only in the perspective of his later work, which makes the cannibalistic heaven, the presentation of Queen Victoria's two sons as Siamese twins, and her Lesbian relationship with Florence Nightingale seem like outrageous alienation effects. But the angle of distortion is so oblique that stylistic innovation is inevitable. The historical episodes are no less fantastic than the sequences set in the cannibalistic heaven, though here Bond is making stage pictures out of satirical surrealism:

Foot of the cliff. The stage is littered with bodies. Some of these are broken dummies. A rope curls round the stage, and under and over and between the bodies. ARTHUR *comes down. He has lost the skull, but the bones are still on his shoulder.*
ARTHUR: Over. Finished. Now I can die in peace. (*He takes out a pistol.*)
FLORENCE *comes in. She is dirty and untidy. She carries the red cross satchel.*
ARTHUR: Why didn't you fall?
FLORENCE: Victoria ran to the edge, so I stayed behind.
ARTHUR: I ought to kill you. It's not fair to leave you out. George would think I hate you. But I've done enough good for one life.

Stylistically both *Narrow Road to the Deep North* (produced 1968) and *The Bundle* (produced 1977) are Brechtian in their unrealistic use of Oriental history to make Marxist points, presenting familiar problems in an unfamiliar perspective. In *Narrow Road*, as in Brecht's *Kaukasische Kreidekreis* (*Caucasian Chalk Circle*), children are used lovelessly as pawns in a power game, while colonials and coolies, priests and pupils are deployed in the manner of his didactic plays. In *The Bundle* the vilification of the unseen landowner and the episodic onstage representation of suffering caused by his unscrupulousness follow the Brechtian pattern. What is lacking is Brecht's poetry and his humour.

Bond's *Lear* (1971)[8] is Brechtian in different ways. It reworks and updates a Shakespearian plot, shifting the focus away from personal issues towards social and political issues, as Brecht did in his version of *Coriolanus*. The King is de-individualized into a representative of military authoritarianism, while the succession of more or less disconnected episodes and the vignette characterization of peasants who appear only briefly are reminiscent of *Mutter Courage*. In his original production of *Lear* at the Royal Court, William Gaskill followed Brecht's Berliner Ensemble by creating locale through foreground object rather than background décor, and in the style of the groupings, lighting, costumes, and overall visual economy.

Robert Bolt has also been stylistically influenced by Brecht, though the underlying preoccupation, unlike Bond's, is with personal relationships. Bolt's first play for the theatre, *The Critic and the Heart* (produced 1957), was conventionally straightforward in its story-telling. In fact Bolt had made a study of Somerset Maugham's *The Circle* (1919), analysing its structure and modelling his own play on it, even tailoring his acts to the same length as Maugham's. In *Flowering Cherry*, which was produced later in 1957, Bolt tried to escape from naturalism by charging some of the speeches with poetic prose and by introducing unnatural effects, as at the end of the play, when the vision of the dying man is translated into a stage picture as the back wall of the set disappears and a cherry orchard becomes visible. (The wall has been painted on a scrim, and the lights are brought up behind it.)

It was in Bolt's third and most successful play, *A Man for All Seasons* (produced 1960), that the style was Brechtian. The action was spread over a long span of time and wide range of places, none of which was established in detail by scenery. There were also devices that produced alienation effects—baskets of props and costumes were lowered from the flies, and the Common Man, a chorus figure, joined in

[8] See above. pp. 20–5.

the action, playing a number of different roles, and changing his costume in front of the audience. He addressed us directly, introducing the scenes, and providing a humorous linking commentary. But whereas Brecht's projections of place-names and plot summaries deliberately interrupt the action by highlighting the division between one scene and the next, the Common Man provides continuity. Bolt's construction is less 'Epic' (in Brecht's sense) than cinematic, with the alienation effects embroidered ornamentally. Far from wanting to make the audience think adversely about the hero, Bolt was inviting the closest possible identification, and in centring so many sequences on More's family life, he was filtering arguments about public issues through private relationships. The main substance of the play is quite un-Brechtian.

Gentle Jack (produced 1963) is Bolt's most original play, not only in structure and style, but also in substance. The idea was to introduce the god Pan into a modern setting, satirizing psychiatric jargon in the way he talks. But the fairy-tale simplification is at odds with the self-consciousness of the characters, who chat to the audience, looking at themselves simultaneously from inside and from outside. At the same time Bolt is trying to integrate too much narrative material into his dramatic action—a story about a multi-millionairess, whose only connection with Pan is her total denial of him, and a story about a shy young man whose personality changes when the god takes possession of him.

Vivat! Vivat Regina! (produced 1970) is like *A Man for All Seasons* in focusing on the private life of great figures in Tudor politics. The unhappiness of the queens appears to derive from the incapacity they both have for normal family relationships. Elizabeth is presented as the archetypal stateswoman, denying the female side of her nature for political reasons, while Mary fulfils herself as a woman at the cost of losing her crown. Elizabeth refuses to have her rival executed without proof of complicity in a plot against her own life, but when Mary is sealed off from contact with her son, she deliberately provides the evidence that will kill her.

Vivat! Vivat Regina! is no less romantic than Schiller's *Maria Stuart*.

Like Robert Bolt, John Mortimer and Peter Shaffer have repeatedly tried to move away from naturalism, but for both of them it has been like a woman they could neither marry nor abandon. They have also oscillated between writing safe plays, catering for the West End audience, and dangerously serious plays, which might have alienated the public they had won. All three writers are prone to perfunctoriness in translating ideas into dramatic action. Their most ambitious plays have not been their best, and their best have not been their most successful.

John Mortimer has concentrated almost entirely on comedy, which he maintains is

the only thing worth writing in this despairing age, provided the comedy is truly on the side of the lonely, the neglected, the unsuccessful, and plays its part in the war against established rules and against the imposing of an arbitrary code of behaviour upon individual and unpredictable human beings.[9]

In his Sixties comedies Mortimer set himself the task of charting 'the tottering course of British middle-class attitudes in decline'.[10] He largely succeeded in capturing the flavour of the fraying gentility he gently satirized. His one-act comedies have considerable charm, which is no disadvantage when the observation is accurate, as in the characterizations of the pathetic barrister and the amiable henpecked murderer in *The Dock Brief* (broadcast 1957, staged 1958). It is a disadvantage when it tilts a play towards sentimentality, as often happens when he infuses a similar likeableness into types he seems less familiar with. His private detectives, his shabby schoolteachers, his publicans, waitresses, speculators, and con men are entertaining, but, unlike Morganhall and Fowle in *The Dock Brief*, they are not distinctive as individuals. Mortimer has endowed too many characters with too much of his own charm. Meanwhile the artificial twists he uses to keep the narrative alive obscure the social comment he intended.

[9] Introduction to *Three Plays* (1958).
[10] Introduction to *Five Plays* (1970).

His first full-length play, *The Wrong Side of the Park* (produced 1960), is more naturalistic than his pieces for radio and television, though it resembles them in depending on the elaboration of fantasies which do not appear to grow organically out of the characterization. The second, *Two Stars for Comfort* (produced 1962), is equally well made but less predictably contrived to end happily. Sam Turner, the owner of a riverside pub, is no less charming or vital than any of the earlier characters, but he is developed in greater depth. Attractive, friendly, easy-going, he is generous enough to take a girl to bed because he feels sorry for her, and then capable of becoming far more deeply involved than he wanted to be. Mortimer had by now freed himself of the compulsion to make every single character lovable, and the unsympathetic neighbours introduce a polarity—which is to figure again in *The Judge* (produced 1967)—between the life-enhancers and the life-deniers.

In both plays repressiveness is associated with the law. In *Two Stars for Comfort* Sam Turner, who knows how to enjoy life and how to share fun with other people, is taken to court and destroyed by people who are secretly jealous of his capacity for *joie de vivre. The Judge* is less naturalistic. The anonymous Judge (who is rather like the penitent judge in Camus's last novel, *La Chute*) is guiltily obsessed with the desire to be judged by the woman he abandoned when he thought she was pregnant. She has a talent for enjoying life, and when he sends his marshall into the shop she runs, she tries to persuade the young man that his life would improve in quality if he gave up the law:

SERENA: This Judge of yours—did he do well at the Bar?

TRAPP: I should think so. Brilliantly.

SERENA: And having done so brilliantly—does he now live a full and amusing life? . . .

TRAPP: Well . . .

SERENA: Does he hold court in the corner of the Swiss Pub surrounded by six mistresses all below the age of twenty? Does he go to Ponza and the Volcanic Islands and Paris when he feels inclined? Does he sing Verdi's *Requiem* while making love? Can he cook miraculous Irish stew?

TRAPP: I don't think so.

SERENA: Or does he sit alone in the evenings wearing striped trousers and listening to the BBC Home Service?
TRAPP: That's rather more like it.
SERENA (*looks at him*): Is that . . . what you're aiming for?

Unfortunately the action depends heavily on its pre-history, which does not come sufficiently into focus, because Mortimer attempts a free-wheeling style. He gives himself more freedom than usual with both time and place, writing a succession of short scenes in different locales, and he lets the Judge address the audience directly. Conditioned by his naturalistic habits, his plotting is ill served by his non-naturalistic structure.

Little could have been predicted about Peter Shaffer's future from *Five Finger Exercise* (produced 1958), which derives much of its plot from Turgenev's *A Month in the Country*, but remains more pedestrian, more oriented to family life, and more melodramatic in its climaxes. In the double bill *The Private Ear* and *The Public Eye* (produced 1962) the second and better piece resembles Mortimer's *I Spy* (produced 1957), which is also about a detective who develops a relationship with the woman he should be shadowing. Shaffer's detective bursts unrealistically but hilariously into life, lifting the play well above the revue sketch level it started on.

The Royal Hunt of the Sun (produced 1964) ambitiously presents the clash between the Incas and sixteenth-century Spain as embodied by the Conquistadores. W. H. Prescott's *The Conquest of Peru* had greatly impressed Shaffer, who had seen a parallel between the Catholic-Inca antinomy and the confrontation between imperialism and communism. In the play, though, he individualizes the conflict, using Pizarro and Atahuallpa, the Inca king, as anti-types, physically, psychologically, and ideologically.

Something of Prescott's style survives in the narrative links, which are ponderous but more solidly, straightforwardly, and, on the whole, simply written than the rest of the dialogue. It is ultimately the texture of Shaffer's writing that lets the play down. It would have required verse, or prose poetry as powerful as Whiting's, to control the resonances emerging out of the wide-ranging references. Shaffer's prose is workmanlike but at best undistinguished and at worst portentous:

You have no eyes for me now, Atahuallpa: they are dusty balls of amber I can tap on. You have no peace for me, Atahuallpa: the birds still scream in your forest. You have no joy for me, Atahuallpa, my boy: the only joy is death. I lived between two hates: I die between two darks: blind eyes and a blind sky. And yet you saw once. The sky seems nothing but you saw. Is there comfort there? The sky knows no feeling but we know them, that's sure. Martin's hope and De Soto's honour and your trust—your trust which hunted me: we alone make these. That's some marvel, yes, some marvel. To sit in a great cold silence, and sing out sweet with just our own warm breath: that's some marvel, surely. To make water in a sand world: surely, surely. . . God's just a name on your nail: and naming begins cries and cruelties.

The farce *Black Comedy* (produced 1965) was based on an idea derived from the Chinese classical theatre—two swordsmen fighting a duel in darkness, but the scene is performed with the stage fully lit. Shaffer's play starts in a blackout, but the audience hears the voices and movements of a young couple chatting and pouring drinks. When a record is played on the gramophone, the sound runs down as if the electricity had fused. The stage is flooded with light but they both stand still as if they are suddenly in darkness. The ensuing farce is extremely entertaining, especially in the Feydeauesque sequence when the young man is trying to move furniture out of the dark flat without letting any of the others guess what is going on. But, as Penelope Gilliatt complained in her *Observer* review, 'there is something else in all games with darkness that might have been developed here, something hallucinatory and out of joint that could have made the play much more startling and touching than it is about people whose usual links with one another have suddenly become damaged and suspect.'[11]

---

[11] Reprinted in *Unholy Fools* (1973), p. 191.

The Battle of Shrivings (produced 1970) is hardly less ambitious than *The Royal Hunt of the Sun*, but it is naturalistic in conception and planned so that the explicit discussion of ideas should be central to the action. The confrontation is again between two philosophies of existence, and again it is worked out in terms of a conflict between two individuals—an apparently saintlike pacifist philosopher, modelled unmistakably on Bertrand Russell, and an anti-liberal, anti-traditionalist poet. The tension holds until the end of the first act, when war is declared between the two men. Theatrically the possibilities are considerable. The two have agreed that the philosopher will be the loser if he ejects the vindictive poet from his house before the weekend is over. Meanwhile his pacifist principles prevent him from retaliating, however violent the provocation. It may have been rash of Shaffer to commit himself to writing dialogue for two such intellectuals, but he ought at least to have succeeded in projecting a theatrical battle between them and in developing both characters during the course of it. However, as in *The Royal Hunt of the Sun*, he fails to fuse the action with the debate, imposing a schematic development on both characters. The philosopher loses his humanist faith, while the poet, like Pizarro, ends up unconvincingly as a convert to the creed of his victim.

Like Bolt's *Gentle Jack*, Shaffer's *Equus* (produced 1973) attacks modern civilization for trying to banish the destructive gods. In Shaffer's play the Panic passions are suggested by the behaviour of a stable boy who blinds six horses which witnessed an abortive sexual encounter he had with a girl. Presented in a complex arrangement of flashbacks, the story plants the incident in a religious context, the horses being equated with gods, partly through associations with events in the boy's past. In production the director, John Dexter, who had played an almost collaborative part in the writing,[12] strengthened the ritualistic and unrealistic elements in the play, using actors in cage-like masks to represent the horses and giving them a chant-like hum to back some of the dialogue. Mime is important in

[12] See interview with Ronald Hayman, *The Times*, 28 July 1973.

the action and part of the audience is seated on the stage, while the whole cast sits in a circle watching. All this ceremonializes the proceedings, as in a church or a law court.

The play's focus is divided between the boy and the psychiatrist who in trying to cure him is fighting a lack of conviction that he will be 'better' when cured:

I'll erase the welts cut into his mind by flying manes. When that's done, I'll set him on a nice mini-scooter and send him puttering off into the Normal World where animals are treated *properly*: made extinct, or put into servitude, or tethered all their lives in dim light, just to feed it! I'll give him the good Normal World where we're tethered beside them—blinking our nights away in a non-stop drench of cathode-ray over our shrivelling heads! I'll take away his Field of Ha Ha, and give him Normal places for his ecstasy—multi-lane highways, driven through the guts of cities, extinguishing Place altogether, even the idea of Place! He'll trot on his metal pony tamely through the concrete evening—and one thing I promise you: he will never touch hide again!

The psychiatric treatment of the boy culminates in a physical climax: in a stylized way the boy re-enacts his blinding of the horses. The analyst is meanwhile himself undergoing a crisis which is presented as a crisis of faith, or lack of it. But with no objective correlative for this side of the action the climax can only be verbal; and, coming after the physical climax, the analyst's outburst is bathetic.

None of Bolt's, Mortimer's, or Shaffer's plays has ever been staged at the Royal Court, where nine of David Storey's received their premieres—a total exceeded only by John Osborne's. But, though the Court, more than any other full-sized London theatre, has been a cockpit for experiment, Storey no less than Bolt, Mortimer, or Shaffer—or Osborne—has repeatedly gone back to naturalism, after repeatedly falling out of love with it.

Like few other English playwrights, Storey regards himself primarily as a novelist, and some of his plays are by-products of the novels. *The Contractor* (produced 1969) grew out of *Radcliffe* (published 1963), where the two main characters get jobs with a firm of tent-contractors, which, like the one in the play, employs several social misfits. *Life Class* (produced 1974) is a variation on an incident in *A Temporary Life* (published 1973). The first two plays, *The Restoration of Arnold Middleton* (produced 1967) and *In Celebration* (produced 1969), are straightforward in their story-telling. *The Contractor* depends less on plot and dramatic action, more on phased changes—substantial but unspectacular—to the stage picture as workmen erect a marquee, prepare it for a wedding reception, and finally dismantle it. The characterization is straightforward, but, like Wesker's *The Kitchen*, *The Contractor* seems to give working activities prominence over individuality and to let the substance of the plot be determined by the place. In fact both plays are naturalistic in the same sense as the best of Zola's novels. Writing to Zola in 1878 Cézanne explained why he preferred *Une Page d'Amour* (1877-8) to *L'Assommoir* (1876-7):

The backgrounds are so painted in that they are suffused with the same passion that motivates the characters, and thus are more in harmony with the actors and less detached from the whole. They seem as it were to be alive and to participate in the sufferings of the living characters.

In these Storey plays climaxes and confrontations are progressively pared down. *In Celebration* is about a family reunion to celebrate the parents' fortieth wedding anniversary, but the dinner party which is central to the plot is excluded from the action, occurring offstage during an interval. The play focuses on events buried in the past, but the predominant feeling is that nothing would be gained by digging them up, that there can be no question of adjusting present attitudes and behaviour to realign them with the past, that the best possibility is of resignation and forgiveness. In *The Contractor*, similarly, the central event of the plot is squeezed out of the action: the marquee is erected for a wedding breakfast, which is eaten during the interval after the second act. The third opens on a tableau of overturned tables, empty bottles, discarded napkins. During the three acts we are introduced, sketchily, to a variety of characters representing different social strata, different attitudes to the way society is developing, different age-groups. There are momentary flares of conflict, and the play is full of germinal stories, but none of them is developed.

Storey's next play, *Home* (produced 1970), moves further away from realism. The setting is not established as a mental home until the first entrance of the two women, and Storey says he did not know, while writing the first long dialogue between the two men, Harry and Jack, whether the action was set in a hotel.[13] He completed the play within two days and he is averse to rewriting or revising, which may mean that he prefers the shape of the play to correspond to the process of creating it, rather in the way that Jean-Luc Godard's films sometimes retain a sequence in which the actress corrected herself or fluffed a line.

In *Home* Storey uses avoidance of confrontation not only as a technique but as a theme. The action is determined by the psychological incapacity of the characters for direct confrontation. The conversations proceed tangentially, avoiding each issue that arises. Relationships are defined more by lack of contact than by contact, more by what remains unsaid and *how* it is left unsaid than by what is said. Much remains ambiguous. As in Beckett and Pinter, identity is partly dissolved by the apparent inability of the characters to remember what has happened to them: their memories and their fantasies become as indistinguishable for us as they are for them. Harry and Jack leave a great many sentences unfinished, a great many trains of thought uncompleted. They also tell each other a great many stories. How much of what they say is true? The question is unanswerable and, since the whole play is a fiction, partly irrelevant. But it is poignant that they flounder with such elegance, that they make so much effort to preserve a façade of dignity, the poignancy resting partly on what the audience has in common with them.

Stylistically *The Changing Room* (produced 1971) is quite different, approximating to documentary realism in

---

[13] Interview in Ronald Hayman, *Playback* (1973), p. 16.

the picture it builds of rugby football players in the changing room before and after the match. Like the central events in *In Celebration* and *The Contractor*, the match is excluded from the action. The changing room, unlike the wedding marquee, is imagined as having a continuing existence (on the same site) both before and after the action, but it comes to life only before, during, and after a game and, as in Wesker's *The Kitchen*, what we see is constructed around two bustling climaxes of activity, while the players change into their rugby clothes and out of them. The focus takes in the thirteen professional footballers, the cleaner, the trainers, the referee, the manager of the club and the chairman. But the play is not entirely about these men. It seems to owe more than any of Storey's previous plays (with the possible exception of *The Contractor*) to a perceptual habit of his, developed by art school training. The wooden benches, the clothes pegs, the towels, the rugby boots, socks, singlets, and shorts, the male bodies in progressive stages of dressing and undressing and the physical actions, including massage and the referee's inspection, all contribute on almost the same level as the dialogue to the impression the play makes. This is in line with Zola's naturalism, except that the significance of the action does not, as in Storey's other plays, rest on some key event that changes the situation of the characters. *The Changing Room* offers a choreography of actions, none intrinsically spectacular, but all watchable and—for most of the audience—unfamiliar. Except for a sequence in which an injured player is helped in from the field there are no incidents which could be called dramatic, and the lack of action helps to focus attention on the individual actions. As in looking at a representational painting, the spectator can concentrate on the quality of the art.

David Storey and David Mercer both trained at an art school. In fact it was the same one—in Wakefield, Yorkshire. Unlike Storey, Mercer has been more of an innovator on television than in the theatre, television being a medium in which a natural, naturalistic or logical progression of pictures can easily be interrupted, not only by departing from the expected sequence but by translating fantasies into screen images and by pushing irrational behaviour into foreground focus. Madness can more easily take possession of the screen than of the stage, and madness is one of Mercer's main preoccupations. In the television play *A Suitable Case for Treatment* (transmitted in 1962 and filmed as *Morgan* in 1965) Morgan Delt, finding reality unacceptable, withdraws into fantasy, and his fantasies encroach on the screen action. A gorilla skin or a zany stare makes less difference to a stage picture than it can to a picture on the screen.

Mercer is like Storey in being concerned simultaneously with psychological and social issues, but he focuses more tightly on individual behaviour. In 1965 he said that 'The only possible revolution is the individual revolution; any expression of individuality, however small, is a revolutionary gesture. Anything, in fact, that helps us to escape from categories. . . Now the "lunatic" fascinated me, I think, because he is the man who, almost by definition, escapes from categories.'[14] His 1965 stage play *Ride a Cock Horse* was about a writer who graduated—through commercial success—out of the working class, only to relapse into infantilism through successive relationships with three women—wife, mistress, whore. There is a strong strain of anarchism in Mercer's plays for both media, but in the stage plays it is more apparent in the behaviour of the central character than in any deviation from naturalistic norms.

In *Belcher's Luck* (produced 1966) there were undercurrents of pent-up appetite and impending disaster in an atmosphere sometimes reminiscent of D. H. Lawrence and sometimes of Lorca. With the crazed mare stamping in the stable and the sun beating down, the yard became like a torrid bullring. But the relationship between the timid, virginal old aristocrat and his loud-mouthed, randy servant, Belcher, was unnecessarily complicated by old-fashioned plotting when an implausible niece arrived to entice Belcher into engineering his master's death so that she could inherit the estate.

Mercer's stage plays have indubitably benefited from the

---

[14] Statement quoted by John Russell Taylor in *The Second Wave* (1971), p. 43.

technical *savoir-faire* he acquired in television, but they are much less adventurous, though *Flint* and *After Haggerty*, which were both premiered in 1970, at least spread themselves uninhibitedly in space and time, without baulking at scenes that might have seemed unstageable—a journey across Europe on a motor bike, a fire that destroys a church, a lecture tour of Budapest, Moscow, Havana, and Prague. Some of these sequences are realized with considerable ingenuity, but in both plays too much of the statement is verbal.

In *Flint* most of the Bishop's lines are spoken into a tape-recorder, while the detective is made to go in for more self-revelatory chatter than probing interrogation. As in Osborne's plays, much of the dialogue is monologue in disguise. If there is any emotional give-and-take it is between the agnostic vicar and the girl who has tried to commit suicide. Though she is pregnant and he is seventy, she finds that he is a better lover than anyone else in her experience. Their relationship is touchingly and tenderly developed, though often, when they seem to be talking to each other, they are wordily pursuing their private preoccupations. Nor is there any irony to focus what is happening: Mercer is too busily involved in entertaining the audience.

But how can you. . . . I'm baffled that you . . . my old skin and bones repel me. I expect you to cringe, sooner or later. (*Pause.*) Stark naked I am an unlovely sight. And yet I have this brutal energy. (*Pause.*) Knobbly feet. Veins like twisted flex. My bowels constantly bubble. One sly fart from me would asphyxiate a cathedral full of solid citizens. The deformities of my kneecaps practically constitute a work of art. Collar bones like doorknobs. (*Pause.*) It is sad that the pubic hair also turns grey in the fullness of time. I am not so much a body as a relic. (*Pause.*) And without God. (*Pause.*) Miss Biggin and I never once undressed. (*Pause.*) We had to preserve, as she so shyly put it: that certain niceness. (*Pause.*) D'you know, I can't remember what it was that took me into the church. (*Pause.*) I remember a vast, shimmering light—and I fear this was not the handiwork of the supernatural, but one of those rare long and golden summers when the born eccentric transcends himself and turns actually potty. In Cambridge.

In *After Haggerty* the construction is stylized to accommodate regular sequences in which a character is either talking out front or talking to an invisible partner. In the first act, each scene in the drama critic's rented flat is followed by a scene in one of the trouble spots where he has been invited to lecture on English drama. Each lecture is an agonized tightrope walk between his subject matter and the current political crisis, each excerpt from it is followed by a one-sided conversation with the critic's working-class father, who is unrepentant in his parochialism. In the second act, when the father takes up temporary residence in the flat, several of the solo spots are taken over by an aggressive American woman, who one-sidedly acts out some of her past experiences with Haggerty, the owner of the flat and father of her child. Ironically, she is still having more of a relationship with him than with the ineffectual critic, who wants her, but cannot find the courage to say so. That Haggerty is kept offstage is both a source of strength and of weakness. His presence is effectively felt through his woman and through the messages he keeps sending the critic, culminating in the news of his death in Africa where he was fighting as a guerrilla. But all the red corpuscles of the play are in Haggerty's bloody-mindedness, so most of the action is too anaemic.

It still seemed possible, after this play, that Mercer would be able to create a larger-than-life-size character, an onstage Haggerty, a successor to Morgan Delt, or a younger, more plausible, less verbal Flint—an iconoclast who would smash his way through all the barriers. Would Mercer be able to synthesize monologue of self-revelation with a dialogue of interaction? And to think simultaneously in visual and verbal terms? *Duck Song* (produced 1974) was stylistically adventurous. Mercer's intention was to find a way of 'visualizing what would happen in the world if everything that makes the world familiar to people was suddenly removed.'[15] But it was naive to assume that this could be achieved simply by removing all the furniture during the interval. Not that the play had been either convincing or suspenseful during the first half. Conception and characterization are Shavian, with an implausible burglar gratuitously and verbosely explaining himself, and a schematic diversity of attitudes arranged among the oddly assorted characters engineered into confronting each other in the house of a rich dilettante painter. The unexplained 'cosmic snap' which removes the furniture also transforms a fully-clothed Red Indian into near-nakedness, but has little effect on the monologuing characters until just before the end, when they quail collectively in face of the death which the future is bringing. The play can hardly have encouraged other writers to take risks.

Like Mercer, Peter Nichols established his reputation as a television playwright before he had any success in the theatre, but unlike Mercer's, his early stage plays are more experimental than his television plays. In *A Day in the Death of Joe Egg* (produced 1967), his first play to succeed in the theatre, he exploits the possibility of making actors talk directly to the audience as they can't on television. The play starts with a shock effect as Bri shouts at the audience:

That's enough! (*Pause. Almost at once, louder*) I said enough! . . . Another word and you'll all be here till five o'clock.
Nothing to me, is it? I've got all the time in the world. (*Moves across without taking his eyes off them.*) I didn't even get to the end of the corridor before there was such a din all the other teachers started opening their doors as much as to say what the hell's going on there's SOMEBODY'S TALKING NOW! (*Pause, stares again, like someone facing a mad dog.*) Who was it? You? You, Mister Man?. . . I did not accuse you, I asked you. Someone in the back row? (*Stares dumbly for some seconds. Relaxes, moves a few steps. Shrugs.*) You're the losers, not me. Who's that? (*Turns on them again.*) Right—hands on heads! Come on, that includes you, put the comb away. Eyes front and sit up. All of you, sit up!

The effect of this particular joke wears off, but the direct relationship which has been established with the public helps to solve the problem of how to write about a spastic child. Bri can talk matter-of-factly about what he and his wife did. The idea for the opening was based on a revue sketch Peter Nichols wrote and performed when he was a teacher; the play succeeds because it maintains its precarious balance between revue entertainment and autobiographical verismo about bringing up a spastic child.

Peter Nichols went on to develop more complicated interrelationships between disparate materials. In *The National Health* (produced 1969), Barnet, the hospital porter, talks to the audience in the same way as a stand-up comedian. His function is partly choric, and he also helps to bridge the gap between the realistic hospital scenes and the fantasy parallel which takes the characters into the world of *Emergency Ward 10* and *Dr. Finlay's Casebook*, television glamorizations of medical routines. The fact of handling such a large group of characters produced problems of perspective; the play had to move briskly and brusquely from a man dying of cancer to the comic inability of a sleep-starved woman doctor to stay awake. The general effect is comic, even if the cost is in shallow involvement with what the dying patients are suffering.

What is a problem of space and numbers in *The National Health* becomes a problem of time in *Forget-Me-Not Lane* (produced 1971), which telescopes twenty years into two hours, with actors making an entrance in the present tense, and making an exit to return several years younger. As in *Joe Egg*, characters talk directly to the audience, comically interrupting an onstage row to make an appeal for sympathy to a neutral spectator. Again the overall effect is comic, but there are serious implications in the abrupt time shifts within the family perspective, as when the husband, watching his thirteen-year-old son observing him quarrelling with his wife, remembers quarrels between his parents. In *Joe Egg* the mixture of comedy and tragedy is sometimes quite acid. In *Forget-Me-Not-Lane* the flavour is always fairly bland. *Chez Nous* (produced 1974) is more conventional in form, and the subsequent plays *The Freeway* (also produced 1974) and *Privates on Parade* (produced 1977) were limited by anxiety about making excessive demands on the audience. Having been content to let *Privates on Parade* become less of a play and more of a musical as the production evolved, Nichols scored the biggest commercial success of his career.

Charles Wood's career offers a complementary illustration of how the British theatre exerts pressures on the emergent playwright, making it almost impossible for him to aim simultaneously at the maximum of commercial success and the optimum development of his talent. Even if Nichols's main talent is for comedy—and some of his best television plays suggest that we should not take this for granted—he could have developed into a playwright capable of less trivial comedies than *Privates on Parade*. But Wood, one of our most talented writers, was forced to work in films because he could not earn his living in the theatre. He has had plays at the Royal Court (*Meals on Wheels*, 1965, *Dingo*, 1967, and *Veterans*, 1972, starring John Gielgud); at the National (*H: or Monologues at Front of Burning Cities*, 1969); at the Aldwych in an RSC production (*Jingo*, 1975); and in the West End (*Fill the Stage with Happy Hours*, 1967), but his only financial successes have been in the cinema.

In *Prisoner and Escort* (the first play in *Cockade*, a triple bill staged in 1963), an almost poetic intensity is distilled, as in Wesker's *Chips with Everything*, out of the vernacular of the armed services, but in Wood's play there are fewer inflations, distortions, and blurred edges. His ironies are sharper, and his rhythms more muscular. He also achieves a good balance among the four characters. Under arrest for urinating on the boots of a visiting German general, the disaffected prisoner is uncommunicative. The escort, a corporal, is conceited, coarse, aggressive. Another private is a dim-witted conformist. The girl, who at first seems attracted to the corporal, switches her allegiance to the prisoner, who is handcuffed uncomfortably to the luggage rack of the railway compartment. But his interest in her ebbs when it emerges that she has been living with a coloured man.

Linguistically more alert and more inventive than most of his contemporaries, Wood gives substance to his dramatic metaphors by fleshing out action with speech that always seems authentic. In his army plays he uses fragmentary memories of experience as a base for complex structures of compelling theatrical images. *Dingo* is by no means realistic.

There is no coherent plot. Characterization is minimal, identity unstable. The play is partly a parody, unpicking the mythology about the desert war that films and novels had built up. War heroes—Montgomery, Rommel, Churchill— are subjected to scathingly anti-heroic treatment, the battle of Alamein being condemned as a slaughterous spectacle staged for the sake of morale and to impress the Americans. The idea that morale can be bolstered by sustained violence is pilloried in the second half of the play, set in a German prisoner-of-war camp, where an officer kills one of his own men *pour encourager les autres.*

The influence of Beckett is not immediately obvious, and the violent action is quite unlike the inaction of *Godot,* while the language is much more savage, but we are reminded of Beckett's play by the brevity of the lines, the arch literariness, the vaudeville skittishness and the comic pointlessness of everything that is being done:

DINGO: The thing about fighting in the desert is that it is a clean war—without brutality. And clean limbed—without dishonourable actions on either side.

MOGG: They say.

DINGO: And there are no civilians.

MOGG: Except me—I'm a civilian.

DINGO: What am I then?

MOGG: Try as I may—I can't see you standing for a number eight bus picking your nose with the edge of your paper.

DINGO: Or barbarity.

MOGG: I've never stopped being a civilian.

DINGO: Or frightfulness.

MOGG: No refinements.

DINGO: I think you are a civilian.

MOGG: I can't deny that—I find the climate most exhilarating. . . .

DINGO: Characteristic of a civilian.

MOGG: You'll find the climate most exhilarating.

DINGO: Take for instance the shit beetle—a more exhilarative sight. . . .

MOGG: And I find excitement bubbling within me. . . .

DINGO: . . . you never shat.

MOGG: . . . at the nearness of the enemy.

DINGO: Characteristic of a civilian.

MOGG: Or a soldier.

DINGO: When did we last brew up?

MOGG: The inevitable brew up.

DINGO: Thumbs up.
MOGG: Desert fashion—the old brew up.

Not that Beckett would have written a scene in which two soldiers try to direct two others into a minefield, or the sequences in which tankman handles the charred corpse of his friend as if it were a ventriloquist's dummy. Wood's savage theatrical images are entirely his own.

H: or Monologues at Front of Burning Cities is another play which uses vaudeville comedy to turn nationalist myth upside down. Set in British India during the 1850s, the play sardonically and devastatingly exposes the disparities between the Christian principles of the mild-mannered Sir Henry Havelock, hero of the campaign against the mutinous sepoys, and the vindictive ferocity of the reprisals he organizes. To Wood it seemed impossible for an intelligent man to be both a Christian and a soldier,[16] and he focuses the absurdity of Havelock's attempt in the quaintness of his language. 'No stones; a piper; no fuss. . . I have not seen the guns go bang so well ever.' Or when a soldier falls dead at his side, 'His was a lovely death, my lambs. He died in the service of his country, some of him upon my boot.' To capture the stresses and cadences of Havelock's speech, Wood writes it out as verse:

Fusiliers, that you are
called the Lambs I know and that
you are the fiercest tiger lambs
ever seen is known to me. There is
a march before us will be Sweat
and Toil and laying down our lives
along the road, I ask you to
whatever comes remember British
ladies; our tenderly nurtured
countrywomen are even now
in Lucknow, Cawnpore,
are emaciated and haggard
parched with drought they are,
most faint with hunger
they must soon be,
whatever the supplies in

[16] See interview with Ronald Hayman, *The Times*, 8 Mar. 1972.

charge they cannot be but
scratch feedings,
even now tender well-born
women face the wait for they
know not what, not soldiers
are they . . . not prepared
and hardened in mind and faith
by sieges stood, forced marches
endured,
they are Innocents!

Written after Wood's screenplay for *The Charge of the Light Brigade* (1968), *H* theatricalizes some of the techniques he had acquired in writing for the cinema, and the assumption behind his next stage play, *Veterans*, is that *H* is being filmed. Set on a film location in Turkey, the play shows two veteran actors sitting around in canvas chairs, waiting to be needed, bored with each other, and failing to sustain the effort to camouflage their boredom. What plot there is turns on an incident in which Laurence D'Orsay (known as Dotty) exposes himself to an ambassador's daughter, but more depends on the mixture of sympathy and bitchiness in the reactions of the other old actor, Sir Geoffrey Kendle, again set out as verse:

I mean, we all know Dotty gets tired
and does these things,
since I can remember. I think it's very
sad the way he automatically flees to his
flies in times of stress,
that's why I always cast him in armour if I
possibly can, or tights . . .

Jingo was less successful. Set in Singapore during 1941, it aims to expose the complacency and incompetence of the British, who are myopically misjudging the danger they are in. Engrossed in adulterous love affairs, tennis parties, and dances at Government House, they cheerfully deride the Japanese as racially inferior. The plot hinges on a situation reminiscent of Noël Coward. Gwendolen has arrived from Bombay with her husband, George, a BBC commentator attached to an information unit, and she finds that her former husband, Ian, a major in the Sappers, is sun-bathing at Raffles Hotel. The triangle turns into a quadrilateral when the commanding officer, a colonel, joins in the pursuit of Gwendolen. His mortification as the British stronghold collapses is very funnily expressed in a bedroom scene, when he abruptly lowers his trousers, asking her to thrash him. Gently wielding a silver hairbrush, she obliges.

Again, Wood shows himself to be extremely sensitive to the way we so often use our language as a means of deluding and reassuring ourselves; thinking in catch-phrases and clichés, we repress the anxiety for which no words come easily to mind, converting embarrassment into cosiness. By deftly arranging phrases and rhythms, Wood mixes the authentic jargon into a theatrically potent brew:

Blackout tonight or there'll be ructions, and leave it off a decent crack or two or there won't half be a to-do on the lawns, caught again looking handsome in the frangipani with egg on one's—one's tomfool John Thomas taking a five-fingered route march.

The British are also seen condescending abominably to the Malaysians who, despite their pidgin English, retain an impressive dignity. Up to a point, language is the subject of the play, but it is not brought into quite the same focus as the adultery and the military incompetence.

Alan Ayckbourn cannot be ranked as an innovative playwright, though he has made some interesting experiments in some of his comedies. In *Mr. Whatnot* (produced 1963) most of the action is wordless. Like Harpo Marx, the eponymous piano-tuner never speaks, but mimes his farcically anarchic way into marrying the daughter of a lord. *How the Other Half Loves* (produced 1969) uses the two halves of the set to represent two living rooms in different houses with contrasting furniture. The two households are linked by an adulterous liaison, and the plot develops a series of confusions involving a third couple used by both lovers for an alibi. In *Absurd Person Singular* (produced 1972) Ayckbourn succeeded in making a girl's suicide attempts into a subject for farcical comedy. *The Norman Conquests* (produced 1973) is an ambitious trilogy, each play involving the same characters, the same time-span, and the same events, but each set in a different part of the house or garden. Allusions in the dialogue are criss-crossed ingeniously so that each play is comprehensible by itself, but each illuminates the incidents of the others by going into detail about what was happening at the same time in a different place.

Having written his early farces under the influence of Feydeau, Ayckbourn began to feel at the beginning of the Seventies that he wanted to put Chekhovian characters into an absurd framework.[17] But Chekhov contrived a brilliantly judged mixture of absurdity and pathos as the framework for the existence of his characters, while Ayckbourn's, well observed and entertaining though they are, get put into situations too patently contrived.

Simon Gray is a playwright of such intelligence that it is hard to explain why he has not been an innovator. *Wise Child* (produced 1967) was the most unorthodox of his plays, centring on a man who is dressed as a woman until just before the end. A naturalistic explanation is provided: he is a criminal disguising himself to evade the police. *Dutch Uncle* (produced 1969) is no less far-fetched: a chiropodist who refuses to sleep with his wife aims to achieve stardom as a criminal with his plan to gas her in a specially prepared cupboard. But, as in *Wise Child*, the situations are exploited mainly for their comic or farcical effect.

The subsequent stage plays, *Butley* (produced 1971), *Dog Days* (produced 1975), *Otherwise Engaged* (produced 1975), and *The Rear Column* (produced 1978), have all been more serious, more realistic, and more like traditional well-made plays.

Christopher Hampton is another playwright with no strong innovatory impulse, though he has not fought shy of unorthodox construction. In *When Did You Last See My Mother?* (produced 1966) and *The Philanthropist* (produced 1970), he tailored his material to theatrical necessity as defined by precedent. *Total Eclipse* (produced 1968)

[17] Interview with Ronald Hayman, *The Times*, 4 July 1973.

was about Rimbaud's relationship with Verlaine, but the characterization of both poets—Rimbaud especially—was subordinated to the necessity of producing coherent and theatrically effective dialogue. *Savages* (produced 1973) is Hampton's most ambitious play and his most committed. The range of the subject matter and the depth of the commitment combined to liberate him from limiting anxieties about whether the play would work in the theatre. He took the risk that critics would accuse him—as they did—of failing to integrate his material, of spatchcocking two plays together, one a didactic play about the mass murder of American Indians in Brazil, the other a personal drama about a British diplomat, Alan West, and a well-born guerrilla, Carlos, who is holding him as hostage.

Undeniably, the scenes involving large groups of characters are not so well written as those between West and Carlos. The script specifies very little about the Indian rituals which are enacted in the background as West, a dilettante poet, recites verse he has written to retell Indian legends about the origin of fire, of the stars, and of music, and about death and survival after it. In production, gauche choreography devised by an anthropologist created an unimpressive theatrical spectacle while at the same time distracting attention from the point that West seriously sympathizes with the Indians. The documentary flashbacks were less inept, though it was too obvious that historical facts were being crammed into the dialogue. In the second act an anthropologist describes methods that have been used to exterminate Indians. Epidemics of measles and influenza have been fomented; large groups of Indians have been transported by air under conditions that killed most of them.

The final ritual is interrupted by a bombing attack. Hampton had wanted to end the play with the pilot and co-pilot of the bomber pouring kerosene over the pile of corpses and lighting a torch—a reprise of the fire image in the first ritual. The production at the Royal Court ended instead with projections on a screen of newspaper headlines about the murder of the kidnapped diplomat, followed by the disappearance of the screen to reveal a heap of anonymous Indian corpses.

Certainly the subtlest writing in *Savages* comes in the suggestion of incipient friendship between hostage and captor, built up through their conversations over the chessboard in the guerrilla hideout. In argument, the sophisticated ageing man scores points off the young fanatic, while both reveal inconsistencies. The Englishman disapproves of the Brazilian dictatorship; the radical likes American girls. The older man, convinced that individual action is politically futile, none the less feels guilty at the extent to which he is an accessory in genocide; the younger man, arguing that action is essential, may subsequently feel misgivings about pulling the trigger on his hostage.

What is most interesting about the play is its way of welding its disparate material together—legend, ritual, documentation and personal relationships. The play is not merely a polemical condemnation of genocide but a balanced theatrical investigation of attitudes that have been adopted towards an insoluble political problem: how to integrate Indian culture into an industrial society. The play makes no simplistic condemnation of 'capitalist imperialism'. Though the guerrillas are anti-capitalist, it is made clear that they would do nothing to help the Indians or to save them from extermination. An English major, who formerly worked for the Indian Preservation Society, argues that since there is now no hope for the Indians, it would save trouble if the extermination could be completed as quickly as possible. An American missionary claims that he has succeeded in changing the lives of the savages by converting them to Christianity. But it will still be necessary to keep them confined behind barbed wire. Hampton's play may not be entirely successful, but at least it represents a genuine experimental attempt at using theatrical terms to work out an important problem. A play that had sided with the well-meaning but ineffectual West, or with the engagingly enthusiastic young killer, would have been much less subtle.

It may have had nothing to do with the critics' reaction to *Savages* that Hampton's next play, *Treats* (produced 1976), was so much more conventional, but if the theatrical climate had been more conducive to experiment, it is doubtful whether twelve years would have elapsed between the London premiere of David Rudkin's *Afore Night Come*, which was the outstanding success of the RSC's first and only experimental season at the Arts Theatre (1962), and his next full-length stage play *Ashes* (1974). The ingredients of *Afore Night Come* are more extraordinary than the way they are put together. The climax is a ritual murder performed in an infected pear orchard by three fruit-pickers wearing black oilcloth, while insecticide is being sprayed down from a helicopter, thin trails of vapour spilling on to the stage as the plane zooms past. The form of a cross is slashed on the victim's chest before his head is severed from his body. But this sensational climax grows organically and credibly out of what has preceded it. The dialogue of the Irish scapegoat verges on the poetic; the others mostly speak Black Country dialect. The obscene jokes, the business of sharpening knives, the brutal attitude to work, the grudging tolerance towards a mentally defective boy, the brooding atmosphere, dark rumbles of primitive religion and the hints (as in Zola and Lawrence) of a sexual relationship between the labourer and the soil—all combine to make the ending seem inevitable.

Ashes is less successful. Unlike *Savages*, in which the relationship between private and public themes is basic to the conception, *Ashes* is flawed by the decision to extend the theme of barrenness from the private sphere to the public, and the construction makes it seem that the decision was taken far too late. The play starts like a documentary, probing uninhibitedly but not unhumorously into the privacy of a couple desperate to have a child. Both partners put themselves trustingly into the hands of the medical profession, which submits each of them to a series of useless humiliations, including sperm counts, post-coital smears, and dutiful love-making in a prescribed position. The bleeding that precedes the wife's miscarriage and the moment of breaking the news of her hysterectomy to her husband are movingly theatrical, while the realism accords perfectly well with the stylized use of one supporting actor and one supporting actress to play a variety of doctors, nurses, adoption-society officials, and a catty girl-friend who conceives all too easily. But though the long speech about the IRA bombing in Belfast is extraordinarily well written, the audience cannot, at such a late stage in the play, be expected to readjust its focus from the couple's private agony to Irish politics. The link between the two themes is metaphorical, not organic.

Heathcote Williams's *AC/DC* (produced 1970) is one of the few English plays to challenge comparison with the work of Beckett, Ionesco, Genet, and Handke. It merits the description *avant-garde* because it is revolutionary in the verbal and visual images it invents. Williams's fundamental concern, like Beckett's, is with the functioning of human consciousness, and the whole ambiguous action of *AC/DC* could be construed as taking place inside the brain. The machines in the amusement arcade of the first act and the video screens in the second, together with the 2,000 photographs of celebrities pasted all over the walls, suggest mental processes and images left on the mind by the media. It is an obsessional play, and the central obsession is with the harmful impact that show-business personalities make on their audience: 'It's no accident that film stars are called stars, you know. They use up the magnetic field to the same extent as any asteroid. Every star that surfaces is using up the Behavioural Field of anything from forty to a hundred ordinary people.' Fame, according to Heathcote Williams, is 'the perversion of the natural human instinct for validation and attention.'[18] The play violently overstates this point: the two main characters, Maurice and Perowne, are schizophrenic, and their schizophrenia—far from being brought into focus—takes possession of the play. The disadvantage is repetitiveness, the advantage a manic energy. Like

[18] Interview with Irving Wardle, *Gambit*, nos. 18–19 (1970).

Beckett, who makes it ambiguous in *Endgame* whether the characters are mad and makes the madness into an advantage,[19] Heathcote Williams is a man of intense personal vision, and in this play he found theatrical correlatives for it.

The opening image is of a boy and two girls having a 'Mongolian cluster fuck' inside a 'Photomaton', bare legs and clothes protruding from under the curtain, flashes of light from this machine and churning noises from the other machines all corresponding to physical sensations. When the coloured girl, Sadie, insists that she wants to 'go solo', we get the first hint that a tug-of-war is going on between individual identity and collective identity. The other two resist: 'We just melted ourselves altogether in a giant gentle atom bomb of sperm and cunt juice.' There are two main streams of verbal and visual imagery in the play, electrical and sexual. Heathcote Williams is concerned to define and articulate the ways, whether obvious or unnoticed, that human beings can encroach on each other's independence. The play takes over the idea many schizophrenics have that other people are malignantly interfering with them by means of electro-magnetic vibration.[20] In *AC/DC* Maurice works to protect Perowne from electrical interference, while Sadie fights to free herself from the possessiveness of her two lovers, male and female, the assumption being that all possessiveness is antiquated and undesirable.

Indispensable though it is, the electronic jargon combines with the schizophrenic distortions to make the dialogue hard to follow, but the climaxes of galvanic action are theatrically compelling. Perowne's epileptic fit is an apt visual metaphor for an uncontrollable discharge of sexual electricity. When Sadie uses a roll of photographs to masturbate with, she is physicalizing the point about the damage stars

---

[19] I have argued this point at length in *Theatre and Anti-Theatre* (1979).
[20] Williams was influenced both by a Hyde Park orator, Billy MacGuinness, whom he described in his book *The Speakers*, and by Dr. Milton Rokeach's book *The Three Christs of Ypsilanti*, a study of three schizophrenics all under the delusion that they were Christ.

do by imposing themselves as subjects of masturbatory fantasies.

The kernel of the subject matter is the possibility of direct brain-to-brain contact, and the title indicates that human beings are convertible. The final and most powerful climax, when Perowne is trepanned by Sadie, is a theatrical image for unmediated contact. As Williams puts it, 'she's really fucking Perowne with her astral dildo.'[21] Trepannation becomes a ritual of purification:

It's only for the top meat, Perowne, Grade A Clears. Occupants of the 35th Bardo, and 7th Astral Plane. It's a Crux Ansata for hooking yourself out of samsara. Out of names and games. It's the biggest by-pass circuit of them all. Speed up your biological clock so that you can contract right out of time, and smash all those second hand pacemakers (*Pointing to the wall of photos*), smash all those electric pricks (*Pointing to the TV*). Clean up all your bad vibrations. Letting the spirits out of the hole, that was the Greek version of it. Thaumaturgic initiation into a higher caste.

Later Sadie's speech and her actions become more rhythmical, her monologue more like a litany. There is more inside our heads, according to Williams, than we can ever express, and Sadie is releasing Perowne by decompressing his skull. At the end he slowly opens his eyes, screams, and, smiling, breaks into a non-cognitive language represented in the script by hieroglyphics.

AC/DC is based on the Artaudian premises that direct brain-to-brain contact is possible, and that the human organism must be changed radically if we are to accommodate ourselves to the future. Having been overloaded with information and with images of the media freaks, Perowne is helped first by Maurice and then by Sadie through a series of rituals to exorcise the spirits that have been possessing him. Sadie, once she has succeeded in 'going solo', is like a witch, and at the same time she is a champion of media democracy:

When my fuckin revolution comes Everybody in the World's gonna be on television ALL THE TIME. THEN there's gonna be an 'Information explosion'. No more names. No more signature artists. No more selective newsreader psychosis. No more selective Beatle psychosis. There's gonna be TOTAL ACCESS.

Maurice is similarly liberated: in Williams's words, he has 'completely smashed up his body image, and doesn't belong to any country at all: he has videotapes of people he's never met playing inside the heads of people he's never met and vice versa'.[22] At one point he cures Perowne of a torsional spasm by urinating over a television screen and plugging a microphone into the set, so that he can superimpose his own commentary while using a magnet to distort all the moving pictures.

In so far as the play succeeds, it not only dramatizes a destruction of barriers between one identity and another, it enforces the experience on the audience. We are sucked into the rituals, both pained and liberated by the trepannation. The new theatre language, said Artaud, must 'use human nervous magnetism to transcend the ordinary limits of art and language to realize actively—that is to say magically, *in real terms*—a sort of total creation, where man has only to resume his position between dreams and reality.'[23] Human nervous magnetism is not only the subject of *AC/DC* but the currency in which it transacts its intimate negotiation with its audience. This is a genuine example of the Theatre of Cruelty.

Of the eighteen playwrights discussed in this chapter, Pinter, Stoppard, and Williams are the only three whose inclinations are not predominantly naturalistic. The others may sometimes deviate from straightforward story-telling, or elaborate it with different forms of stylization, but the main impulse is narrative, and tension never depends on dissolution or merging of individual identity, but usually on separation and contrast.

Not that we still believe in the premises of naturalism. In

[22] ibid.
[23] Manifesto for the Theatre of Cruelty (1932), reprinted in *Le Théâtre et son double* (1938).

Le Naturalisme au théâtre Zola called on the playwright to imitate Balzac and to abandon abstraction in favour of 'direct observation, accurate anatomy, acceptance and representation of what *exists*'. In reacting against the Romantics, the Naturalists were embracing the scientific method formulated by Claude Bernard.[24] Experiment and observation would disclose the pattern behind seemingly unrelated phenomena. Individual behaviour from moment to moment would be studied in relation to environment and heredity. A work of art's only merit, said Zola, was 'that of exact observation, of the more or less profound penetration of analysis, of the logical concatenation of the facts.' In the nineteenth century it was still unthinkable that there might be no concatenation, and it was possible to believe, as Chekhov did, that 'A writer must be as objective as a chemist.' Modern science has taught us to be sceptical both about our capacity for objectivity and about the possibility of making causal connections. Nor can we go on assuming, like Zola, that any accurate account of any human experience will contribute to our understanding of both nature and human nature. We no longer believe in either as a self-consistent entity.

What the critic must decide, then, is whether the fragmented naturalism that survives is poisoning the mainstream of modern drama, or whether it is floating along harmlessly, felicitously jolted by Brechtian, Artaudian, and Beckettian currents. It has become clear that theatre can accommodate powerful anti-illusionistic elements without ceasing to entertain primarily through illusion. Can we not argue that realistic story-telling is still a legitimate pleasure, even if we have rejected the view of reality prevalent when realistic art evolved? We could even reinforce our defence of traditional story-telling by making the point that the idea of experimental art derives from naturalistic scientism: the work of art as laboratory experiment.

Of the fifteen playwrights who are not temperamentally inclined to experiment how many can be said to be at their

[24] Cf. his *Introduction à l'étude de médecine expérimentale* (1865).

best when writing most naturalistically? In Wesker and Storey the naturalism is deep-rooted: *The Kitchen* and *The Changing Room* are demonstrations of a relationship between environment and action, while *Roots*, despite the irony of the title, is no less naturalistic in its concern with heredity and environment. Osborne is at his best in *The Entertainer* and *Inadmissible Evidence*, using stylization to gain extra resonance for a straightforward story, whether the stylization works anti-illusionistically (as in *The Entertainer*) or not (as in *Inadmissible Evidence*). Bond did his best work when writing naturalistically. Like Pinter and Wesker, he lost urgency in losing touch with his working-class roots. As his language and preoccupations became more literary, the rhythms in his dialogue became less lively. Joe Orton was at his best in *Loot*, which is tolerable because the illusion is imperfect and the language stylized.

The best plays of Bolt (*A Man for All Seasons*), Shaffer (*The Royal Hunt of the Sun* and *Equus*), and Mortimer (*The Dock Brief*) are not their most naturalistic, but in each case the stylization serves not to destroy the illusion but to heighten it. The same could be said of Mercer's best stage play (*After Haggerty*), but Nichols's most striking effects in *A Day in the Death of Joe Egg* and in *The National Health* do depend on shattering the illusion by stepping into revue technique. Like John Arden, Charles Wood and David Rudkin have both approximated to verse drama, arguably moving away from the ephemeral and superficial in doing so.[25] The best comedies of Simon Gray and Alan Ayckbourn succeed in looking more naturalistic than they are. In *Savages* Christopher Hampton's departure from naturalism produced such good results that it seems a pity he did not stay away longer. Had the theatrical climate been less inimical to experiment, perhaps he would have done.

One of the pressures that have helped to suffocate experimental theatre in this country[26] is cultural egalitarianism, as evidenced by the popularity of the word 'elitist' as a

[25] See above, pp. 64–8 and 72–3.
[26] I shall discuss the others in chapter 4.

term of abuse. Obscurity is not a *sine qua non* of experiment, but freedom is: the writer must feel free to make demands on his audience, and in England the endemic fear has been that only an intellectual elite is willing to have demands made on it. The most important young Austrian and German experimental playwrights, Peter Handke, Wolfgang Bauer, Rainer Werner Fassbinder, and Franz Zaver Kroetz, are all left-wingers, but they have not considered it anti-democratic to write difficult plays. In England Heathcote Williams has been virtually unique in risking what he calls 'obscurantism', and his reason for taking the risk was idiosyncratic. In 1966, watching a London performance of his one-act play *The Local Stigmatic* (premiered in Edinburgh 1965), he saw a woman in the audience having a fit during the beating-up sequence and shouting out 'Stop it.' 'Somehow I was afraid of that infective threshold. Having felt it I wanted to make the new play totally self-contained.'

3 The politics of hatred

'Being a bastard won't always be so bad,' argues the heroine of David Hare's 1978 play *Plenty*. She wants a working-class boy to give her a baby without any prospect of a continuing relationship with her. 'I wouldn't bet on it,' he answers, but she insists: 'England can't be like this for ever.

The point of the title is that the prosperity which ensued on wartime austerity was hollow and unsavoury. The action moves backward and forward between 1944, when Susan was working for British Intelligence in occupied France, and 1962, when she is certifiably mad. After the war, says David Hare, 'Britain was a hard place to use the skills and energy gained when people were at full stretch. It's what happens to idealistic people who have been used.'[1]

Susan is one of the best roles written for an actress since Brecht's *Mutter Courage*, and the play is Hare's best so far, but it is seriously flawed by its awkward division of focus between rotting psyche and rotten society. The implication is that the main causes of Susan's deterioration are social. We see her mouldering with discontent in a well-paid advertising job, and making rebellious gestures (like stealing food) when she is working for the 1951 Festival of Britain. After marrying a young diplomat, she discharges her indignation about Suez in the presence of an ambassador; later she threatens a high-ranking official that she will shoot herself unless her husband is promoted. Her freedom from inhibition, her determination, and her outspokenness are self-defeating and destructive, but she seems not only more courageous but more admirable than anyone else in the play. David Hare's attitude to her is obviously ambivalent, and this is damaging because it disqualifies him from providing

[1] Interview in *Sunday Times Magazine*, 9 April 1978.

us with a perspective. We are being invited to judge Susan without sufficient evidence. War naturally offers an outlet for aggressiveness which needs to be restrained in peacetime, but in so far as the play is arguing that her wartime experience is the cause of her subsequent difficulties, it fails to substantiate its point, and in so far as it is using her as a yardstick to hold up against the moral corruption of postwar England, it is perverse. The progressive abnormality of her behaviour makes her increasingly useless as a norm. Her frustration cannot but be read as a criticism of the society she lives in, but the portrayal of that society is fragmentary and inadequate. The characterization of the husband is pale and shallow. Apart from Susan, the only character in the play to engage David Hare's sympathy is Alice, her girl-friend, another deviant, who lives on the periphery of society, first as a writer and later as a social worker. But this is a badly written part, and the relationship between the two girls is never convincing. Alice's need for Susan's money is evident enough, but we never learn what it is in Alice that Susan likes or needs.

The paradox of the play is that it presents Susan as an individual, interesting because of the way her mind works, but that it seems to be written from the anti-individualistic premises which are still fashionable. Private behaviour must be explained in terms of social, political, and economic pressures. The Marxist theatrical theories Brecht evolved in the late Twenties and early Thirties had no effect on the English theatre until the late Fifties, but their influence is still dominant. In 1959, Kenneth Tynan, the critic who primed our theatre for Brechtian infiltration, wrote that 'Arnold Wesker came closer than any other English dramatist to demonstrating that socialist realism was not a dogmatic formula but a uniquely powerful means of conveying sane theatrical emotion.'[2] In the middle Fifties, when Marxism was having little effect on intellectual opinion in England, it seemed very odd that Brecht should think the quality of a play depended on whether it was useful in provoking social change. Shortly before he died, he professed

[2] Review reprinted in *Tynan Right and Left* (1967), p. 13.

himself unable to judge Sartre's 1947 play *Les Mains sales* because he hadn't re-read it since Kruschchev's speech at the 20th Party Congress.[3] But by the middle Seventies socialist realism had become the norm. For D. H. Lawrence it had been axiomatic that since art was the best means of telling the truth about life, nothing could possibly matter more than being an artist; our socialist realist playwrights are on the whole less interested in being artists than in precipitating social change. Trevor Griffiths has told an interviewer that if he believed he could do more towards changing Britain by working 'on the streets or in the political parties', he would give up writing plays.[4]

John Arden's book *To Present the Pretence* (1977) helps to explain what has happened to him since he wrote his early plays, which are unquestionably works of art, whereas the priority in his later work is propagandistic. It was in 1967 that he entered decisively into a working partnership with his wife, Margaretta D'Arcy, whose instincts as a dramatist, he writes, 'have tended to operate in the reverse order to mine. She will think of a *subject* that requires to be dramatized: and will relate it to the conditions of the time and the potential audience to be sought for it. Only then will the idea of a story to embody the theme, and a style to narrate the story, become uppermost in her mind.' In the early plays, his method had been to start with a story that appealed to him. He allowed himself this luxury only in two radio plays—*The Bagman* (1970) and *The Pearl* (1978)—both written independently.

The Island of the Mighty (produced 1972) is the best of the plays the two have written together, but this collaboration was complicated by Arden's thirty-year involvement with the material. He was only fourteen when he discovered Malory's *Morte d'Arthur*. In 1953 he made his first attempt at a play on the subject, linking the survival of pre-Christian ideas and rituals with the rivalry between British military

---

[3] Ronald Hayman, 'A Last Interview with Brecht', *The London Magazine*, vol. III, no. 11 (November 1956).
[4] Television interview with Benedict Nightingale, cited by Oleg Kerensky in *The New British Drama* (1977), p. 201.

leaders which handicapped their resistance to the Anglo-Saxon invaders. After writing another version of the play in 1955, Arden returned to the idea ten years later, stimulated by a BBC commission to write three television plays to be screened as a trilogy. The three plays involved him in so much work that they were not ready until 1969, when the BBC no longer wanted them. That year, while he was in India with his wife, he invited her to collaborate on reconstructing the three television scripts for the stage. She felt (as she later wrote in an Introduction to the play) that what was lacking in the scripts was 'a sense of precise sociological realism—there was altogether too much importance given to picturesque historical detail and not enough consideration accorded to the fact that even during the most frenzied periods of economic and political disturbance people still have to go on living.' The Ardens were both influenced by the performances they saw of Indian folk dramas and the Jatra plays of Bengal, which incorporate complex mythological and historical material. Yet, said Margaretta D'Arcy, 'the style of the staging was simple and direct, the main emphasis was always towards a strong and vivid story-telling, and where the plot became too diffuse for "dramatization", the action was hurried forward by means of rapid verse-narrative, songs, and instrumental music.' This acceleration may be all very well when the stories are thoroughly familiar to the audience, but the Arthurian legend is not sufficiently well known. In the process of writing and rewriting the play, expanding it into three television plays, contracting it for a single evening in the theatre, collaborating with Margaretta D'Arcy and incorporating material from sources rooted in contrasting cultures and attitudes, Arden accreted narrative material and stylistic devices which pulled him in different directions.

One result is the imbalance of satire and sympathy in the characterization of King Arthur. Some of the confusion probably dates back to the point at which Arden developed him into 'a disruptive figure, both reactionary and revolutionary at one and the same time.' In the final draft he is more reactionary than revolutionary, but he is being used to represent several different disciplinary systems. The Ardens did not want to condone 'imperialism', but they could not help revealing a reluctant sympathy for his up-standing, paternalistic strength, buttressed by the twin disci-plines of Roman militarism and Christian self-denial, how-ever repressive these both were. The play comes closest to solving the technical problem when Arthur's inconsistencies are in focus. We see him, for instance, taking Gwenhwyvar for himself instead of letting Medraut marry her, and al-though he insists that his motives are partly political and entirely altruistic—she is too dangerous a woman for his nephew to subdue—he is also prompted by lust and the desire to prove himself virile enough to take a young wife.

Another structural weakness results from the failure to integrate the theme of poets and the way their paymasters force them to make history into legend. Harnessing Marxist arguments to Arthurian horses, the Ardens were at pains to show that the poets who originated the legends were them-selves deviating from the truth, corrupted by pecuniary pressures. But it is unhistorical to represent the territorial princes as so concerned about their image that they needed poets as public relations officers. The overdevelopment of this theme and the excessive stage time given to the poets probably reflects a basic uneasiness.

Like *Armstrong's Last Goodnight*,[5] *The Island of the Mighty* is fundamentally concerned with the effects of social organization on rudimentary human energy. The qualities of amiability and aggressiveness that had equipped Johnny Armstrong to be a leader in an anarchic, primitive society, did not help him to survive in the new civilization, which was more rational, better organized, better disciplined. In the Britain of a thousand years earlier, the movement was in the opposite direction: no longer in the tight administra-tive grip of the Roman Empire, the sixth-century Britons were lapsing back into tribalism. In the Ardens' play, social and economic issues are sometimes represented by individ-ual events, as when a cowman is shown to be suffering

[5] See above, pp. 14–15.

from the depredations of both rival armies on his livestock, and sometimes, as in Shakespeare's history plays, the points are made in scenes of argument involving the King. Arthur's nephew, the Prince of Strathclyde, who feels threatened by the Wild-Cat Picts, has sent his chief poet Taliesin to denounce them at the council, while they have sent a priestess, who is also a goddess, as their ambassador. The dispute illustrates a point Arden had already made in *Armstrong's Last Goodnight*: that Christian evangelism can be used as a smokescreen to cover territorial acquisitiveness. Noblemen in Strathclyde have been grazing their cattle on hills that the Picts had always claimed as their own, trying to convert any Picts they encountered.

As the narrative proceeds episodically, incidents involving new characters are presented simply, immediately acquiring an appeal like that of a ballad. But what is gained by simplicity is lost when political messages are stuffed anachronistically and insensitively into situations which cannot accommodate them, as when a Bondwoman pleads for the solidarity of the oppressed

Look forget you are a nobleman. If you must live a life of fighting, why not fight in defence of me? There are so many like myself everything that is ever done in the name of God or good order becomes done against us. The best thing of all would be if you could make friends with Garlon. He is not always clever but he has had dealings in his time with every outlaw gang through the breadth of the forests of Britain. What—yourself and himself—good friends and good fighters— you could soon have a thousand men!

Like Arden's plays, Edward Bond's have become more political, but while Arden is no longer using historical analogies to comment on the present situation, Bond, after his two plays set in contemporary England, *The Pope's Wedding* and *Saved*, began to pick vantage points which were more remote—historically or geographically or both. *Early Morning* (1968) is a Victorian extravaganza which works like a monstrous distorting mirror to show the present an image of itself in disguise as a Victorian grandparent:

VICTORIA: Albert, dearest, where have you been since breakfast?
ALBERT (*kisses her cheek*): My love.
VICTORIA: Thank you. You've cured my headache. (*She makes a formal address.*) Our kingdom is degenerating. Our people cannot walk on our highways in peace. They cannot count their money in safety, even though our head is on it. We cannot understand most of what is called our English. Our prisons are full. Instead of fighting our enemies our armies are putting down strikers and guarding our judges. Our peace is broken. You know that the Prince of Wales poses certain constitutional questions. Because of this the anarchists and immoralists say that the monarchy must end with our death, and so they shoot at us. They are wrong. Our son will follow in our footsteps, with his brother at his side, and in time his son will follow him. Our line began at Stonehenge, and we shall not fall till Stonehenge falls. We shall not abandon this kingdom to anarchy. That is why our son will have a normal marriage. His bride will be Miss Florence Nightingale.

Narrow Road to the Deep North (1968) and *The Bundle* (1977) are both set in the Japan of an indeterminate period between the seventeenth century and the nineteenth, but as in *Early Morning*, the real subject is the possibility of resistance to authoritarian oppression. Like Brecht in his Chinese plays, Bond takes advantage of the audience's unfamiliarity with the subject matter, transposing history into parable. But his play about Shakespeare is equally unhistorical. Stylistically *Bingo* (1973)[6] is more realistic than *Early Morning*, but Shakespeare is presented as if he gave up writing during the last years of his life because he could not cope with the guilt he had accumulated at failing to intervene in the class war of the early seventeenth century. He does nothing to stop two landowners from enclosing some common fields, and by contrasting his passivity with the active resistance of men who are illegally filling in trenches dug by the landowners' men, Bond tries to convict Shakespeare of complicity in the cruelty and injustice which he witnesses. In fact he obliquely condemned it in his plays, as in Lear's mad speeches on the heath. To suggest that Shakespeare was making an existential choice, giving his support to an oppressive and unjust society, is to blame him

[6] See above, pp. 23–4.

for failing to think in a twentieth-century way, but, as in *Early Morning*, Bond likes to outrage his audience by slinging theatrical mud at a national monument. If the fictitious playwright in *Bingo* had been given a different name, the play would have made less impact.

In *Narrow Road to the Deep North*, as in *Early Morning*, Bond launches his ironic attack on imperialism and evangelism by putting an apologia for both into the mouth of a monstrously caricatured female. Talking about the cruelty of the tyrant Shogo, the missionary Georgina says:

It didn't work, because it left people free to judge him. They said: he makes us suffer and that's wrong. He calls it law and order, but we say it's crime against us—and that's why they threw spears at him. So instead of atrocity I use morality. I persuade people—in their hearts—that they are sin, and that they have evil thoughts, and that they're greedy and violent and destructive, and—more than anything else—that their bodies must be hidden, and that sex is nasty and corrupting and must be secret. When they believe all that they do what they're told. They don't judge you—they feel guilty themselves and accept that you have the right to judge them. That's how I run the city: the missions and churches and bishops and magistrates and politicians and papers will tell people they are sin and must be kept in order. If sin didn't exist it would be necessary to invent it. I learned all this from my Scottish nanny. She taught our Prime Minister, the Queen, the Leader of the Opposition, and everyone else who matters. They all learned politics across her knee. I am enjoying this conversation.

In *The Bundle* Bond returns to the same starting point: at the beginning of each play the poet Basho uses his dedication to the contemplative life as an excuse for refusing to adopt a baby which has been abandoned on the banks of a river. In *Narrow Road to the Deep North* the baby grows up into the tyrant Shogo; in *The Bundle*, the baby grows up into a revolutionary, Wang. Himself confronted with the same choice, whether to save the life of an abandoned baby, Wang flings the bundle into the river, and the audience is expected to approve of his decision. If he becomes sentimentally involved in bringing up a child, he will be distracted from his revolutionary activities. The assumption is that once the existing social order has been replaced by a new one, wealth will be distributed so equitably that parents will never again be forced by poverty to abandon their children. In fact Bond is building his parable around the commonplace argument used by those who try to justify terrorism: human life must be sacrificed in the violence which is indispensable if society is to be changed.

Arden and Bond are not the only playwrights to have sacrificed artistry to activism. In 1958 John McGrath was a twenty-three-year-old undergraduate reading English Literature, when his interesting first play, *A Man Has Two Fathers*, was produced in Oxford. *Why the Chicken*, which attracted considerable attention when it was produced by the Oxford University Dramatic Society at the Edinburgh Festival in 1959, prefigured McGrath's subsequent development: a well-meaning middle-class social worker tries to get herself accepted by a gang of working-class youngsters. In spite of the plot's dependence on an offstage climbing incident (in which she causes the death of a boy who has tried to rape her), the action effectively penetrates the girl's almost loving involvement with a class that must ultimately reject her, however bravely she commits herself, however close she comes to winning the love of the ringleader.

The equivalent figure in the all-male *Events While Guarding the Bofors Gun* (produced 1966) is a well-meaning young Lance-Bombardier with mild, middle-class manners. He ruins his chances of promotion by compromising with the men who are in his charge, letting them break the rules by going to a NAAFI canteen while on guard duty. He then has to depend more on their good will than on his ability to impose his authority, if he is going to keep them sufficiently under control to satisfy the officer who comes around to inspect the guard. In *Why the Chicken* the differentiation between members of the group had depended partly on varying degrees of aggressiveness, while McGrath had been making his first exploration of the relationship between aggression and self-destructiveness, a theme which figured again in *Events While Guarding the Bofors Gun*.

The twenty-nine-year-old Gunner O'Rourke in the later

play is described as 'tall, wild and desperate. An Irish bandit with a terrifying deathwish, a desperado whose humour, viciousness, drunkenness and ultimate despair come from deep within. To say he is bitter is to underestimate his scorn for himself and all life. He is uncontrollable, manic.' After taking savage delight in exposing the weakness and inconsistency of Lance-Bombardier Evans, he jumps drunkenly out of a window. Eventually he kills himself by falling on to a bayonet. The final irony is that Evans, with no hope left of promotion, is himself provoked into gratuitous aggression. Kicking the body, fully aware that it is dead, he tells O'Rourke he is on a charge. According to McGrath, the play is about 'two kinds of consciousness, one of which is going along with the rules of the game—not very good at them, but getting better all the time—and the other, the root-consciousness of the oppressed, who are driven to futile, alienated work, and who react quite understandably, with a kind of passionate abandon, abandonment of purpose, and fall back on to immediate, slightly irrational and self-destructive emotions.'[7] Violent masochism has great appeal to the playwright who dislikes the social *status quo*: O'Rourke has an affinity with Susan in Hare's *Plenty* and with several of Stephen Poliakoff's characters.[8]

Something of the same theme survives in the one-act play *Plugged in to History*, the best in a series of five plays written for the Everyman Theatre, Liverpool, and produced there in 1971 under the title *Unruly Elements*. This was the year in which McGrath founded the touring company to which he has since devoted most of his working energy, called the 7:84 Theatre Company because 84 per cent of Britain's wealth is said to be in the hands of 7 per cent of its population. The company's declared objective is 'raising consciousness. Primarily of the working class and its potential allies.' McGrath says:

The perceptions of Marx, Engels, Lenin, Trotsky, Luxemburg, Gramsci, Mao Tse-Tung and the rich traditions of working-class

[7] Interview in *Theatre Quarterly*, nos. 19–20 (1975).
[8] See below, pp. 118–25.

thought and experience in Britain cannot be ignored. They affect the way we phrase our questions, and provide the tools for tackling them. . . . There are many ways of working for socialism, ours is simply to go around providing entertainment, theatre, that raises the issues that the media ignore but which the working class recognizes as the real issues; that provides information that is needed in a shape that makes sense of it; asserting values that oppose capitalist values; questioning assumptions that are too readily accepted; unfolding something of the dialectic of our time, so it can be grasped; insisting that every one of us is responsible for his or her destiny, and must tear that responsibility from the hands of the ruling class who have taken it away from us.[9]

In 1972 the company toured three of the one-act plays, together with another, also by McGrath, called *Hover through the Fog*. The plays were performed at Edinburgh during the May Day rally and in Glasgow at McNeill's Heavy Engineering Factory while it was occupied by the workers.

In most of these plays, as in most of the work McGrath has since written for his company, the fusion of personal and socio-political themes is perfunctory and unsuccessful. He claims that his 'growing political consciousness' has been 'allied to a growing feeling for individual human beings, with all the contradictions that alliance involves.'[10] The final phrase indicates uneasiness, but it is only in *Plugged in to History* that he manages to draw creatively on his insecurity. Again he introduces a female *alter ego*, a masochistic middle-class mother involved in a park-bench encounter with an aggressive labourer who has been jilted by a middle-class girl. The climactic revelation is that she would like him to inflict physical pain on her, as he has on the girl-friend who hurt him mentally. The device of having the mother, Kay, read imaginary news items from invisible papers suspended in mid-air succeeds in planting her private agony in the public context of contemporary history's wholesale infliction of pain on masses of people with no such masochistic need. As she says,

[9] *Theatre Quarterly*, nos. 19–20.
[10] Statement in *Contemporary Dramatists*, ed. James Vinson (1977), p. 534.

When I read my papers, I feel plugged in to history, I feel the course of events coursing through my veins. I feel taken over, crushed, by many many men. I feel occupied, a house, squatted in, defiled. I feel like a deserted ballroom being defecated in by a halted army. I feel like South America after the Yankees have finished with it, like Dresden after the bombing. I feel like a shed full of cats. I feel like a midnight zoo. I feel like a clump of trees outside a barracks, full of soldiers in rough khaki having under-age village tarts. I feel like Pompeii the next morning. I become a human news-tape, mile after mile of me, torn out, ripped off, abandoned. Do you know why? Do you begin to? It's because I feel everything, all the way through me.

Neatly linking public events with private suffering, the play expresses McGrath's impatience with those who feel no sympathy for victims of the Yankees in South America or victims of the RAF bombers in Dresden. But the characterization of Kay depends too much on her impersonal, newspaperish recital of worldwide horrors:

Paris. A girl student who prefers to remain anonymous, testified on oath after her release from Beaujon prison yesterday, that she had seen a young boy student after he had been tortured by the French CRS. He was running screaming up and down the corridor between the cells, she claimed, urinating uncontrollably, his penis beaten to a pulp by police batons. Beaujon prison authorities questioned the authenticity of the report, saying they had not received any complaints from the boy.

Even the comedy works like an impersonal sneer, while there is no substantiation for the assumption that the working classes are more concerned than the middle classes about the sufferings caused by injustice all over the globe. Some such implied generalization underlies a great many political plays. An argument is concealed under the dramatic action, which illustrates it—invariably by recourse to special pleading. The playwright is always free to pick the examples that fit his case, and to present them as if they were typical of a whole class or a whole society.

Since 1972 McGrath's work has been not only more didactic but more eclectic. His objective has been to contribute as much as possible towards the destruction of capitalism, and in appealing to working-class audiences from Orkney to Plymouth, he has restored to caricature and stereotype, drawing freely on the existing mythology which has been bred out of resentment and fantasies of revenge against monstrous landlords and black-hearted employers. At the same time he has come to lean heavily on other playwrights, including Brecht and John Arden. *Serjeant Musgrave Dances On* (produced 1972) sharpens the political edge and blunts the subtlety of Arden's play. *Fish in the Sea* (produced 1973) borrows from Brecht's *The Caucasian Chalk Circle* and Arden's *Island of the Mighty*. In *Yobbo Nowt* (produced 1975), which is about the political education of a working-class mother, McGrath is patently indebted to Brecht's dramatization of Gorky's *The Mother*. Though *Yobbo Nowt* is thin in dramatic texture, McGrath's old talent can still be seen flickering through his dogmatism, particularly in scenes depicting family life. In both *Fish in the Sea* and *Yobbo Nowt* there are flashes of warmth, tenderness, and humour in the dramatization of working-class suffering.

But why write a new version of a play that was only thirteen years old? The suggestion came from Arden himself. The 7:84 Company produced the Ardens' agitprop play *The Ballygombeen Bequest*, and it occurred to Arden that Serjeant Musgrave could be made into a paratroop sergeant coming back from Derry after the killings of Bloody Sunday. Arden, in other words, was suggesting a reversal of the policy he had adopted in moving back to the nineteenth century for an imaginary parallel to a recent incident in Cyprus. In any case, *Serjeant Musgrave's Dance*, as Arden wrote it, would have been largely incomprehensible to the audience that was coming to village halls for productions by the 7:84 Company. As David Hare has said, 'Literary values cannot survive on the road'.[11]

The progress of David Hare and Howard Brenton from touring with Portable Theatre[12] to writing for the National has been like an inverted image of John McGrath's progress

[11] Interview with Peter Ansorge, *Plays and Players*, vol. XIX, no. 5 (February 1972).
[12] See below, pp. 129–30.

from London to touring in the North of England and in Scotland. Nevertheless, the work of Hare and Brenton would not have developed in the way it has without the formative experience of catering for an audience that was not habituated to theatregoing. In script and *mise en scène* they had to find means of grabbing the public's attention and then holding it.

Hare directed the original production of Howard Brenton's 1969 play *Christie in Love*, which is like a Donald McGill postcard transformed into an abrasive theatrical satirization of Establishment attitudes. The writing is aggressive but economical and original. The action cuts jaggedly from image to image, impact to impact. What the characters say is relatively unimportant, as we see at the beginning when the two policemen come out with a gratuitous series of dirty limericks and jokes. The strategy is to make them seem no less obnoxious than the murderer, who at least has the temerity not to nurse unacted desires. As the policemen try, coarsely, to understand and condemn what Christie has done, the moral norms of our society seem to be under attack. Our standards are being corroded by the smells issuing from under the floorboards of the house at Rillington Place.

The best of the early Portable plays justified their stridency, but the company was soon going through a phase in which both writers and directors were producing deafening effects for their own sake and deceiving themselves about their motives for wanting to shock. *Lay-By* (produced 1971) was a co-operative play written at David Hare's suggestion and based on a prurient newspaper report on an alleged motorway rape and the ensuing trial. Trevor Griffiths, who had cut out the report, was one of the six writers Hare enlisted to collaborate with him. The others included Howard Brenton, Stephen Poliakoff, and Snoo Wilson, who directed the play. One of the characters, a pornographic photographer, was seen setting up obscene poses. Later on a girl confronted with a man wearing an enormous pink dildo bit off the end. In the final scene naked male and female corpses were daubed with paint by two hospital attendants, who then stewed them in a large vat and started to eat them. In a 1972 interview Howard Brenton said, 'A really great outburst of nihilism like. . . the last act of *Lay-By* is one of the most beautiful and positive things you can see on a stage.'[13]

The aggressiveness of *Lay-By* and the early plays by Hare and Brenton cannot be explained entirely in terms of their need to keep a firm grip on audiences in village halls. As Hare said in 1972, 'Our aggressiveness is immensely conscious. I suppose it stems from a basic contempt for people who go to the theatre. It gets worse when we get near population centres. I loathe most people as individuals and, *en masse*, I find people particularly objectionable. But the aggression isn't entirely spurious. We wanted to pick up the medium of theatre and shake it by the scruff of its neck.'[14]

The first Brenton play to receive a large-scale production was *Magnificence*, which was seen at the Royal Court in 1972. Story and style are no less aggressive or misanthropic than the attitude expressed by one of the squatters:

I loathe us. I loathe all the talks we had. That we'd really do it. Come down to the people whom it really hits. . . . And do it for them. I loathe us, I loathe our stupid, puerile view of the World. That we have only to do it, that we have only to go puff, and the monster buildings will go splat. . . . I loathe us, I loathe what we've descended to do here. . . . Our domesticity. . . . Ten days with the fleas and the tin opener lost, never for once questioning. . . . That we are in any way changing the bloody, bleeding ugly world. . . . Direct action! For us it's come down to sitting on a stinking lavatory for ten days. . . .

As so often in political plays, the audience's sympathy is conducted towards the radicals by introducing reactionaries who behave obnoxiously. In the first act a vicious bailiff kicks a pregnant girl in the stomach; in the second we meet a pair of homosexual Tory politicians known as Alice and Babs. Alice is a Cabinet minister, Babs an ex-Cabinet minister. Amusing though it is, their cynical conversation makes them quite unsympathetic enough; Brenton could have dispensed with the implausible tirade in which Babs

[13] Interview with Peter Ansorge, op. cit.
[14] ibid.

denounces Alice as 'a fascist. . . a peculiarly modern, peculiarly English kind of fascist. Without regalia. Blithe, simple-minded and vicious. I hate you. You scare me sick.'

The action culminates in a confrontation between Alice and an ex-squatter, Jed, who has become more militant since the girl's loss of her baby. He tells Alice: 'It would be magnificent to have you bleeding on the lawn.' After tying a mask of gelignite around Alice's head, he lights the fuse. The explosive fails to detonate, but when Jed throws it to the ground he blows himself up as well as his victim. As Howard Brenton has conceded, the structure of the play is badly marred because he realized too late that though he admired Jed's ferocity, the character who embodies what he calls 'the play's wisdom' is Cliff, a boy who is given very little to do or to say.[15] Cliff is appalled at Jed's death because of the waste. Instead of destroying himself he should have been prepared to work more gradually for the revolution.

Brassneck (produced 1973) was written by Hare and Brenton in collaboration. One of the advantages of regarding the bourgeoisie as a cohesive group and capitalism as a monolithic system is that it seems possible to expose the corruption of the whole by exposing the corruption of the part. Another advantage is that quasi-religious zeal puts high-octane fuel into the energy tank. Focusing on one imaginary Midlands town, Stanton, *Brassneck* takes a wide time-span (1945–73) and a wide-angle view of commercial and municipal malpractice. By telling the story of three unscrupulous generations in a family which rises in provincial society, Hare and Brenton manage to incorporate knowing references to a wide variety of techniques for cheating in the power games of sex, finance, and local politics. After arriving in the town with a suitcase full of money, Alfred Bagley manoeuvres his way into the Masonic Lodge, winning the good will of the most influential citizens. The story is carried forward to the equally reprehensible manipulations of Alfred's nephew, Roderick, an architect with

[15] Interview with Ronald Hayman, *The New Review*, no. 29 (August 1976).

no qualifications, and of Roderick's son, Sidney, who goes into the heroin trade. (In Hare's play *Knuckle*, produced 1974, the ruthless capitalist will deal in armaments—drugs and weapons having become the two symbols of corrupt trading.)

Among the lines in *Brassneck* which assert that capitalism is doomed, one of the most striking is Sidney's prognostication: 'The day is coming when businesses will be run like high security prisons.' This image may have grown out of the same germ as Brenton's *The Churchill Play* (produced 1975), which is the best of the full-length plays he has so far written, making more impact and containing better dialogue than either *Weapons of Happiness* (produced 1976) or *Epsom Downs* (produced 1977). The high-security prison is a British concentration camp, which bears Churchill's name. The action, which is set in 1984, might have been more plausible if Brenton had forgotten Orwell's title and opted for the remoter future. We are required to believe that by 1984 a Conservative—Labour coalition will have passed a new Industrial Relations Act so that militant trade unionists and disorderly pickets can be treated as conspirators and isolated in camps. This time the theme of terrorism is treated only obliquely. The camp is run, brutally and murderously, by the army, who have been conditioned, we are told, by being made to shoot down strikers and Irish terrorists. A melodramatic climax is provided for the third of the four acts by the death of a refractory prisoner who has been 'dumped' by the camp guards.

Brenton's vision of the future derives much of its theatrical cogency from the partly valid fear that our liberty is daily being eroded. But his theatrical imagery is more powerful than his arguments. In an earlier Brenton play, *Hitler Dances* (produced 1972), children playing on a bomb site are terrified to see a dead German soldier coming back to life. *The Churchill Play* opens very strikingly with another image of resurrection: four servicemen are grouped in front of a stained-glass window around a catafalque draped with a Union Jack. They are scared when they hear knocking from inside the coffin, which starts to tremble as Churchill's voice booms out. Finally he bursts his way out, swirling the Union Jack and holding an unlit cigar. But a change of lighting reveals that the stained glass is made out of flimsy paper, and that the action belongs to a play within a play. Churchill's face is a mask, which is pulled off to reveal the puckered hang-dog face of a forty-five-year-old Derby man. The play is to be put on by prisoners in the camp for a visit from a group of MPs.

The resurrection image grows out of the fear that fascism is not dead, and in Brenton's play Churchill is implicitly blamed for the indifference to human liberty which will lead by 1984 to the existence of concentration camps in Britain. His achievement as a war leader is derided: it was the people of Britain who won the war. And one of the main climaxes is built up from a sequence of the prisoners' play set in wartime Peckham by the edge of a land-mine crater. When Churchill comes to see the damage, Uncle Ernie tells him, 'We can take it. . . . But we just might give it back to you one day.' This is later distorted by history into 'We can take it, guv'. Brenton's mind is closed to the possibility that anyone could really have wanted to say 'We can take it, guv.' So far as he is concerned, the war never eclipsed the class war.

The best-written scene is one in which a hardened, sadistic, fascistic sergeant is scornfully defying a liberal-minded officer, insulting him even by the way in which he keeps calling him 'sir', and threatening him with a reminder that officers have been killed by men. In this scene Brenton is able to create theatrically exciting tension, partly because his sympathies are divided: he likes the defiance of authority but disapproves of the man who is being defiant. In the scene with the Members of Parliament his sympathies are not divided, while his satire is perfunctory and heavy-handed. Jonathan St. John is a caricature of willingness to accept compromise; Julia Richmond is a villainess who climbs with implausible speed on to her hobby-horse. She would like insurgents to be controlled by confinement in a white box and by brain surgery.

Trevor Griffiths's *Comedians* is another politically motivated play about aggressiveness, but it is more interesting than *The Churchill Play*, partly because Griffiths, who seems genuinely worried about the relationship between artistry and aggression, is telling a story which brings the problem into focus. The central conflict involves three attitudes. Eddie Waters, who is running a class for would-be comedians, represents the values of liberal humanism. 'Hate your audience,' he tells his students, 'and you'll end up hating yourself.' The talent-spotter Challenor, who can help them into their first professional jobs, feels nothing but contempt for audiences. According to him, the art of the comedian is escapist art. 'I'm not looking for philosophers,' he says. Nothing matters except success, which can be achieved by giving the public what it wants. 'We can't all be Max Bygraves, but we can try.' The antagonism between Waters and Challenor is initially defined in terms of the class war. Waters tells his students that he never joined Challenor's Comedy Artists' and Managers' Federation because he'd been a union man all his life and believed that 'No comedian worth his salt could ever "federate" with a manager.'

Later the antagonism is developed in terms of conflicting attitudes to the function of the comedian, and here it becomes obvious that Griffiths is simultaneously writing about the function of the playwright and the function of art. The real comedian

dares to see what his listeners shy away from, fear to express. And what he sees is a sort of truth, about people, about their situation, about what hurts or terrifies them, about what's hard, above all, about what they *want*. A joke releases the tension, says the unsayable, any joke pretty well. But a true joke, a comedian's joke, has to do more than release tension, it has to *liberate* the will and the desire, it has to *change the situation*.

He is opposed to all jokes based on prejudice:

A joke that feeds on ignorance starves its audience. We have the choice. We can say something or we can say nothing. Not everything true is funny, and not everything funny is true. Most comics *feed* prejudice and fear and blinkered vision, but the best ones, the best ones ... illuminate them, make them clearer to see, easier to deal

with. We've got to make people laugh till they cry. Cry. Till they
find their pain and their beauty. Comedy is medicine. Not coloured
sweeties to rot their teeth with.

This is partly a camouflaged apologia for didactic art, but
it is grooved into the plot. Performing in a bingo hall to
audition for Challenor in front of an audience, some of the
budding comedians will make last-minute changes to the
acts they have prepared, steering away from Waters's principles towards Challenor's.

The third attitude is represented by Gethin Price, the
most talented pupil in Waters's class. After arriving in a
mood of prickly restiveness, he stays aloof from the easy
camaraderie of the others, and when it is his turn to speak
the tongue-twister 'The traitor distrusts the truth', he is
accurate but puzzlingly vehement. That he is no longer
willing to accept his teacher's principles is revealed when
he recites an obscene limerick:

> There was a young lady called Pratt
> Who would hang from the light by her hat
> With a frightening cough
> She would jerk herself off
> By sinking her teeth in her twat.

And when Waters is out of the room, Gethin cruelly mi-
mics him in front of the class. In the climactic audition sequence, Gethin's deviation from the act he has been working
on with Waters is not impelled by any wish to please
Challenor. Dressed and made up to look like a football
hooligan with a clown-white face, he spreads a filthy handkerchief on his shoulder to perform a routine with a tiny
violin, which he finally smashes by stamping on it. After
performing a series of Kung Fu exercises, he ends the act
with a venomous monologue addressed to two beautiful
dummies in evening clothes. They both have 'a faint unself-
conscious arrogance in their carriage'. As if they could
have responded, and as if he had the right to feel insulted
by being ignored, he alternates between exaggerated
chumminess and self-righteous resentment, gradually becoming more aggressive. He then starts telling them dirty
jokes: 'You can laugh, you know, I don't mind you laughing.

I'm *talking* to you. . . There's people'd call this *envy*, you know, it's not, it's hate.' When he produces a flower from his pocket and pins it between the girl's breasts, a dark red stain starts to spread over her white dress. Finally he picks up another tiny violin to play four bars of *The Red Flag*.

Griffiths's intention is to make Gethin's performance approximate to the style of the Soviet clown Grock. 'Thing I liked was his hardness,' says Gethin, who has read about him in a book. Waters pronounces the act 'brilliant', and for the play to succeed fully, it is necessary for the audience to endorse this verdict, and to agree when Gethin tells Waters that without hatred there is no truth:

You think the truth is *beautiful*? You've forgotten what it's *like*. You knew it when you started off, Oldham Empire, People's Music Hall, Colne Hippodrome, Bolton Grand, New Brighton Palace, Ardwick Empire, Ardwick Hippodrome, the Met, the Star in Ancoats . . . the Lancashire Lad—you knew it then all right. Nobody hit harder than Eddie Waters, that's what they say. Because you were still in touch with what made you. . .hunger, diphtheria, filth, unemployment, penny clubs, means tests, bed bugs, head lice. . . Was all *that* truth beautiful? (*Pause.* WATERS *stares at him, blinded.*) Truth was a fist you hit with. Now it's like. . . now it's like cowflop, a day old, hard until it's underfoot and then it's. . . green, soft. Shitten. (*Pause.*) Nothing's changed, Mr. Waters, is what I'm saying. When I stand upright—like tonight at that club—I bang my head on the ceiling. Just like you fifty years ago. We're still caged, exploited, prodded and pulled at, milked, fattened, slaughtered, cut up, fed out. We still don't belong to ourselves.

This explanation may seem suspiciously emotive, but the speech that follows is still more rhetorical. Accused of having gone soft, Waters defends himself by describing a visit to Buchenwald: 'It was a world like any other. It was the logic of our world. . . extended. . . .' But he did not find it merely repulsive: something inside him lovèd it so much that he had an erection. Once again Nazism is being invoked to prove that hatred is necessary and admirable.

It is not very plausible that a man like Waters, who objects so strongly to jokes that depend on prejudice against coloured people, the Jews, the Irish, or women, would be so impressed by a performance centred on prejudice against the upper middle class. Gethin is confusing class hatred with truth, and Griffiths is unaware of his mistake. Another fallacy built into the scheme of the play is that the only alternative to being an escapist comedian is to be a didactic comedian. In so far as vaudeville is serving as an analogy for art, the schema is misleading. But the main flaw in the play is not a flaw in its argument: it is the flaw that results from structuring the action on an argument. With Challenor as spokesman for escapism and Waters as spokesman for the view which is intended to seem antithetical, Gethin's view is meant to emerge as more acceptable than either. But because he cannot trust the audience to be as impressed as Waters is by Gethin's performance, which forms the play's natural climax, coming at the end of the second act, Griffiths adds a third, which culminates in the discussion between Gethin and Waters. All this is disappointingly static by comparison with the second act.

At the same time, Griffiths has missed a good opportunity to dig more deeply into his central ambivalence about love and hatred. In his 1970 play *Occupations*, Kabak, the Soviet agent, tries to reprove Gramsci for loving the working classes. 'You can't love an army, comrade,' he says. 'An army is a machine. This one makes revolutions. If it breaks down, you get another one. Love has nothing to do with it.' Gramsci argues that nothing is more relevant than love:

I came to the masses with the same mechanical views of them, and my own relation to them, as you have just propounded. Use them. Tool them up. Keep them greased. Discard them when they wear out. But then I thought, how can a man bind himself to the masses, if he has never loved anyone himself, not even his mother or his father. I thought, how can a man love a collectivity, when he has not profoundly loved single human creatures. And it was then I began to see masses as people and it was only then that I began to love them, in their particular, detailed, local, individual character.

Griffiths's *The Party* (produced 1973) is set during the Parisian students' rebellion of 1968, and its main climax occurs when John Tagg, leader of a British Trotskyite party, reveals that his cadres in Paris are not going to support the students:

A revolutionary faction cannot afford to be. . . romantic. Because of the *folie de grandeur* of a handful of petty-bourgeois anarchists who're making the running, hundreds upon hundreds of brave young men and women are having their bodies mangled right now by the armed might of the bourgeois state. . . . Our section walked away from the barricades before the major confrontations occurred. In my view, they took the correct decision. Because such a confrontation could only result in defeat, even rout. It lacks revolutionary perspective, and those who promoted it. . . Mandel and his cronies. . . are, in the objective sense, enemies of the working-class revolution in France.

Implicitly the play condemns this attitude as deficient in the kind of love which Gramsci felt towards people both individually and collectively. Tagg's unloving and unlovable cynicism provokes the central character in *The Party* to lend money to his younger brother, who wants to start a business. But in *Comedians* Griffiths adopts an anti-love position.

So does Howard Barker. For him

The stage is the last remaining arena for the free assault of our society. It is the sump to which our poisons and our malices, our despairs and terrors, drain. It is not a place for reconciliation or relief. It is not a dark place rumbling with laughter or a padded private place for the touching of hands, but a granite crucible in which conflict and collision strike dangerous, disconcerting sparks. . . . Nothing is unacceptable on the stage except the breakdown of communication. Nothing is incredible or unlikely. It is the world which is incredible and unlikely, and it is the business of the theatre to show the agony we experience in failing to come to terms with that.[16]

So far Barker's plays have all opened the throttle quite widely to hate and aggression, without ignoring the question which is formulated at the end of *Stripwell* (produced 1975), when a criminal, carrying a sawn-off shotgun, breaks into the house of the judge who has sentenced him

[16] Statement in *Contemporary Dramatists*, op. cit., p. 65.

to a year's imprisonment. Falteringly, the frightened judge makes a case for compromise in a reasonable society, and the argument seems likely to secure his survival: 'We have to draw a line between what we feel. . . here (*He touches his heart.*)—our first impulse—and what is practical. (*Pause.*) Don't we?' After an almost intolerable pause, the thug wanders out through the French windows, only to return, shotgun levelled at the guardian of middle-class morality. 'No,' he yells, and shoots.

Much of Howard Barker's earlier work focuses on the tug-of-war between individual libido and social superego. *Cheek*, his first play to be produced (1970), justifies its title and sets up its tensions by taking its tone from the thrusting cockiness of the central character—outrageous by the standards of conventional behaviour, natural by the standards of a healthy boy's sexual appetite. In *Edward: the Final Days* (produced 1971), a polemic about Heath, the inventiveness is clogged up with cheap indignation, cartoonish parody, and simplistic argument.

Claw (produced 1975) is more sophisticated than any of his earlier plays in its treatment of the no-man's-land between private lust and public images. The central character is a pimp, and it was amusing to make him spectacled and virginal. The creation of Noel Biledew acted like a counter-blast to the Jimmy Porter mythology: working-class boy makes middle-class girl, bold, sexy pleb versus timid, passive, effete female. Fed up with being victimized, Noel Biledew takes the name 'Claw', but fails to learn from his mother's husband, a convert to communism, that he should save his anger for his class. His career as pimp begins badly. He offers a schoolgirl to a policeman, who buys her for a pound, but retrieves his money by punching Biledew in the stomach. He learns from his mistake and becomes very successful, pimping for a Cabinet minister, until he presses his luck too hard and his omnipotent client decides that he must be eliminated.

Much of the theatrical imagery is extremely vivid, and much of the comedy is lively, especially in the second act, when the Cabinet minister's ex-chorus-girl wife mischievously seduces the unattractive Biledew. The distended third act is worst, resting—and nearly going to sleep—on the premise that the Establishment can survive only by employing ex-hangmen and ex-terrorists to staff a 'mental hospital' where they rub out social misfits who could discredit the governing elite.

Stripwell is less didactic, less dependent on stereotypes, better constructed. It is also more consistently entertaining because the comedy is more organic. It is characteristic of Barker—as it was of the Marquis de Sade—to use a criminal as an incarnation of the integrity that the judge lacks. But the thug is wisely kept offstage throughout the central action, which occurs during the twelve months when he is safely in prison. If the writing is less heavy-handed than in *Claw*, it is partly because Barker is now prepared to explore his ambivalence towards the main characters, though none of them is particularly likeable. The old survivor of the first Labour government has no warmth or idealism left in him, Stripwell's wife is tiresomely fixated on her cynical son, the gogo dancer is loyal only to her own greed for experience, and we are meant to lose sympathy with Stripwell when he informs on his son, telling the police that the boy is smuggling drugs in elephants' vaginas.

Like Brenton's *The Churchill Play*, Barker's *That Good Between Us* (produced 1977) presents an alarmist picture of a future Britain in which liberal impulses go on flickering feebly in a few kindly individuals while the government gets its way by ruthlessly applying totalitarian methods, using its army like the Nazi SS and turning a blind eye when trouble-makers are 'dumped'. The female Labour Home Secretary makes gestures of holding on to the principles of democracy—'We don't want to end up like Brazil, do we?' 'Don't do violence to language or you will end up doing violence to people.' But in each of her arguments with the chief of her spy ring, she allows herself to be persuaded that the current crisis is too bad to be brought under control without a little secret killing.

Much of the writing is on the level of a script for some such television series as *The Trouble Shooters*. Unlike the notion of using elephants' vaginas for drug-smuggling, the situations in *That Good Between Us* seldom lack surface plausibility, but the pressures that the characters are putting on each other do not stand up to serious analysis, because Howard Barker has not given them any. The villain of the piece is Ronald Knatchbull, the secret service man. The scheme of the play requires him to keep eroding the vestigial decency of Mrs. Orbison, the Home Secretary. Barker is not interested in the psychological question of who or what puts pressure on Knatchbull, and he often resorts to unexplained melodramatic coincidences, as when Knatchbull turns up, with an Alsatian on a lead, at the moment that Billy McPhee is about to rape a woman whom he and two other men have dragged out of a stationary car. Anxious to prevent Knatchbull from seeming too diabolical, Barker makes him dote on his paraplegic daughter. But the sequence in which we see them together is melodramatic. Flying a kite for her on Wimbledon Common, he trips over the dead body of a soldier, Private Hayman, a man who has been tortured and killed at Knatchbull's orders because he tried to warn the leader of a left-wing conspiracy in the army that the Special Branch was in the process of penetrating it. 'Make daddy a daisy chain,' says the nonplussed Knatchbull, trying to distract his daughter. And 'I blame the television. All this viewing. If I was a better father I'd stop it. Make you read.' But Barker is not content to let the scene rest on ironies like these. The corpse starts to talk. When Knatchbull tries to make out that he knows nothing about how the soldier died, the dead man contradicts him. When the girl asks questions which her father tries to evade, the corpse answers them: 'They tied me to a chair. Poured petrol up my nostrils. Twisted combs in my hair. . . I have never known such pain.'

The most interesting character is Godber, the quiet, unscrupulous young man who wants to win stardom as a government spy. Otherwise, he has no ambitions. 'You could put my wants into a matchbox. The rest is rat's piss so far as I'm concerned.' He tries to seduce Mrs. Orbison, and, immediately after failing, succeeds rather implausibly in seducing her radical daughter by telling her that he failed with her mother. Rhoda is not even discouraged when, visiting him in his room, she finds a milk bottle full of urine. 'You cleanly educated people,' he grumbles. 'You end up fetishistic for snot.' She explains: 'I came because there were so many excellent reasons why I shouldn't. And I was sick to death of them. . . . When things were all right here, I was very keen on chaos. As a fire to be gone through, for a specific betterness on the other side. But now we are in chaos I find. . . I just like chaos.' He answers: 'Looking in the abyss. And if it makes you dizzy, it makes you dizzy. . . . That is all you need to be a star. . . stand outside their decency.'

Jimmy Porter would seem to be a very decent young man by comparison with Godber, but if we are in any doubt about the extent to which Howard Barker is identifying with his disaffected hero, the question is partly answered by the reference to theatre in Rhoda's next speech. At university she took part in a play. During the action a man from the front row was dragged up on stage, undressed, roughed up, and robbed. At the end, he clapped with the rest and left without even asking for the return of his pigskin wallet. Howard Barker is trying, successfully, to entertain us by roughing us up.

One of the troubles with this kind of play is that none of its potential is ever fully developed. It was noticeable in *That Good Between Us* that the playwright tended to end each sequence just as it was becoming interesting. Godber's attempt to seduce Mrs. Orbison, for instance, ends abruptly with her saying, 'Now please go.' There is no concern with his embarrassment in getting himself out of the room, no hint of how she would behave when left alone again. Not that the play would necessarily work better if the abortive scene were developed: like melodrama and television serials, it works perfectly well, within its own terms, by jumping from one violent climax to the next. Too much energy has gone into contriving the *coups de théâtre*, not enough into organizing the relationship between them.

David Edgar, who had his first plays produced while he

was working as a reporter for a Bradford newspaper, believes that what he calls 'bourgeois, individualistic psychological values' are inimical to the kind of theatre he is interested in—'radical, alternative Marxist theatre'.[17] 'Deliberately,' he writes,

the new Theatre must be almost everything the old Theatre is not. It must be serious in content, but accessible in form. It must be popular without being populist. It must be orientated towards a working-class audience. It must be temporary, immediate, specific, functional. It must get out of theatre buildings. It must be ideological, and proud of it. It must be celebratory (try to convince the Catholic Church that there's no function in 'preaching to the converted'!). It must not be escapist; it must take our times by the throat . . . the central artistic problem is portraying people's behaviour as a function of their social nexus rather than individual psychology.[18]

Though he uses the word 'artistic', his insistence on the words 'temporary', 'immediate', and 'functional' make it clear that he is not concerned whether his plays are works of art that will survive.

Edgar's attitude to conventional bourgeois culture is articulated in his play *The National Theatre* (produced 1975), which is set in a dressing room occupied by three actresses. The first to arrive is Ella, who works through some lines from Chekhov's *Three Sisters* as if she is about to perform in it. But she changes into a very un-Chekhovian costume, and after the second girl, Marie, has arrived, it emerges that the three actresses are appearing in a striptease show. Though the play has moved tangentially away from *The Three Sisters*, it seems as though a disillusioned parallel is intended: the proprietor of the club is known as the Colonel. And the function of the play's title is not merely to mislead. The main point is that *louche* voyeurism is representative of the consumer attitude to the arts prevalent in bourgeois Britain. The play was written in the final phase of Harold Wilson's final stint as Prime Minister, and though

[17] Discussion on 'British Playwriting in the Seventies', *Theatre Quarterly*, no. 24 (1976).
[18] Statement in *Contemporary Dramatists*, op. cit., p. 236.

he is not savaged as Heath was in Howard Barker's *Edward: the Final Days*, the closing sequence of *The National Theatre* introduces a parody of Wilsonian rhetoric when a character who had previously seemed to be an assistant stage manager talks into a microphone, appealing to the nation for austerity and restraint. 'Not a year for self, but a year for Britain.' The speech is counterpointed against a routine of vulgarly choreographed striptease to imply that creative energy is being misspent on catering for a minority of rich perverts and Japanese tourists in mackintoshes.

Meanwhile considerable tension is developed out of personal relationships. Marie, a working-class girl, has been having an affair with the Colonel, unaware of his preference for another girl-friend. Though Ella puts on an act of not being middle-class, her behaviour still accords with her accent. A failed actress, she goes on doing voice exercises and entertaining fantasies about success. Eileen, another working-class girl, arrives late with bruises all over her body, having been raped by her husband. Her problem is how to camouflage the bruises for the striptease. At the climax Marie and Eileen are both sacked; Ella is kept on because of her classy accent. Not that she speaks during the show.

Like Margaretta D'Arcy, though, David Edgar is not interested in story for its own sake, and, like Howard Brenton, he sees it as his main duty to warn audiences that the possibility of a totalitarian Britain is not as remote as it was in 1948, when Orwell was writing *Nineteen Eighty-Four*. *The Churchill Play* was set only nine years ahead of the date it was produced; David Edgar's 1973 play *Operation Iskra* was set in 1977, so it is already unproducible. After starting like a documentary set in the future, it develops into something more like a political thriller. Most of it is entertaining, with a few patches of dullness due to over-hasty incorporation of material Edgar discovered during his conscientious research into such subjects as legal infringements of liberty in Britain, and how to make your own bomb. Some of the violent climaxes—such as the explosion in the dress shop—are contrived without enough relevance to the rest of the action, but a considerable theatrical momentum is developed as the plot comes to grips with the theme of terrorism. The terrorists are all character-ized sympathetically but fairly convincingly, and the con-flict between them depends more on clashing personalities than clashing ideologies. David Edgar's 1976 play *Destiny* was prefigured most directly in the creation of the least convincing character, a Tory brigadier who lectures at a university and runs an anti-terrorist unit in the police force, covertly recruiting it from the army. Two of the girls who appear to be working for one side are secretly working for the other—here the writing owes a lot to espionage films— and the climax comes when the Brigadier is captured and finally shot by a terrorist splinter group. This scene suffers by comparison with Christopher Hampton's 1973 play *Savages*, which treats its killing with much more sensitivity.

Destiny is better integrated, never making sacrifices or compromises for the sake of immediate dramatic effect. Ambitiously conceived, painstakingly researched and in-geniously constructed, it is a disturbing piece of writing, which centres on an analysis of the factors that pressure people into joining the National Front (or the Nation For-ward Party, as it is called in the play). The second scene of Act Two realistically reconstructs a meeting of a Midlands patriotic league which is about to join forces with Nation Forward. Heterogeneous grievances are voiced. The secre-tary of the league thinks that coloured schoolchildren will infect the whites by spreading parasitic worms. A middle-aged woman complains that the Young Conservatives 'often seem more socialist than the socialists themselves' and that there is no trade union to protect the people who have to live on fixed incomes. The wife of a polytechnic lecturer grumbles about mortgage rates and immigrant students who don't study seriously. A shop steward in a foundry voices his resentment of Indian immigrants who are com-peting for jobs with English factory workers. The sequence is quite convincing in its demonstration of the way dis-parate grievances like these can be raked together by a party that offers scapegoats and promises constructive action.

The play is aimed primarily at an audience which went neither to West End theatres in the Fifties nor to the Royal Court in the Sixties. It is a journalistic play, a dramatization of material yielded by the kind of research that might have gone into the preparation of a television documentary, and in so far as it succeeds in the theatre, it succeeds by setting up in rivalry to television, at the same time as taking advantage of the sense of community that didactic plays can offer an audience of believers. In the same way that *Comedians* can be fully effective only if the public is willing to accept the gospel of class hatred that Gethin preaches, *Destiny* depends on the audience's willingness to accept its prognosis. But the characters who speculate most persuasively about the future are the crypto-fascists:

KERSHAW: I'm sorry, Lewis. Just can't see it in those terms.

ROLFE: Why not?

KERSHAW: I suppose—a basic faith in people's reason.

ROLFE: Reason?

KERSHAW: Loyalty.

ROLFE: To what?

KERSHAW: To Britain. No, that's meaningless. The National Interest.

ROLFE: Whose? Whose loyalty? (*Slight pause.*) Come on, whose loyalty? The miners? Dockers? Students? Irish? Bla-cks?

KERSHAW: Now, Lewis—

ROLFE: I will tell you. Whose commitment to the National Interest matters. Whose loyalty is both vital and, now, under strain.

KERSHAW: Yes, well?

ROLFE: The lower middle classes.

KERSHAW: Continue.

ROLFE: Whose loyalty is bought. By giving them: the independence property affords. A social status, noses just above the Joneses. And the feeling that they're part of something wider, nation, if you like, its destiny. All right?

KERSHAW: Right.

ROLFE (*Increasingly emotional as the speech goes on*): And, on all counts, they've been betrayed. Their property no longer secure. Their status, in our age, increasingly irrelevant. And in the place of national destiny, we've given them. . . You see, Frank, it's not true we've lost an Empire, haven't found a role. We have a role. As Europe's whipping boy. The one who's far worse off than you are. Kind of—awful warning system of the West. And to play that role, we must become more shoddy, threadbare, second-rate. Not even charming. Quite unlovable. And for those—the people that I come from—that is a betrayal.

The imperial theme is presented very cleverly by starting the action in India on 15 August 1947 when British rule is coming to an end. The scene introduces an elderly colonel, a major, a sergeant, and an Indian servant. Back in England we meet the colonel's nephew, who becomes a Conservative candidate, the ex-sergeant, who becomes secretary of the patriotic league and later a Nation Forward candidate, and the ex-major, who is rejected as Conservative candidate and eventually attracted to Nation Forward. The Indian servant becomes an immigrant factory worker who will be active in picket-line brawling.

Some of the climaxes do not depend at all on personal relationships. There is a very effective scene in which the ex-sergeant, who has become an antique dealer, tries to argue with the Pakistani representative of a big property developer who has done a deal with the council over a compulsory purchase order, so that nothing can save the shop from being made into a zen macrobiotic luncheon take-away. There is another scene—possibly derived from Brecht's *Der aufhaltsame Aufsteig des Arturo Ui* (*The Resistible Rise of Arturo Ui*, written 1941, produced 1958), in which the Hitler character is coached in oratory by an actor—showing how Turner is rehearsed by the leaders of Nation Forward for his election speech. But the Labour Party candidate's relationship with his wife is developed, less convincingly, in terms of political disagreements:

SANDY (*kneels beside* CLIFTON, *takes his hand. Very gently*): Bob. Once—you may remember, you said, about the party. Why you're in it.
CLIFTON: Mm?
SANDY: You said, despite—oh, all the right-wingers, all the selling out, you said at least, at least there was a chance of changing things. Of, really, changing things. You could have joined some tiny, fringe, some two-horsed revolution, kept your ideas pure, you said, but at the price of never being any real use to anyone. You wished to be of use, you said, with all the compromise, retreat, the scorn that that implies.
(CLIFTON *looks at* SANDY.)

And that struck me as being rather brave.
(CLIFTON *smiles at* SANDY.)
Let's go to bed.
(*Slight pause.*)
    CLIFTON: OK.

In fact none of the private relationships is developed as effectively as in *The National Theatre*. Certainly, temperamental clashes at a picket line are as legitimate a subject for drama as temperamental clashes in the drawing-room or the bedroom, but the characterization in *Destiny* suffers because David Edgar is more concerned to deploy the results of research than to explore material in the process of writing. The action is too schematic to admit any investigation of individuality, while his only interest in storytelling is to illustrate his thesis.

Wreckers, which was written for the 7:84 Company and produced by it in 1977, is rougher still, both in its aggressiveness and in its construction. Again, more energy seems to have gone into the research than into the writing, both, this time, being done collectively. The question of the relationship between law-breaking and immorality had arisen in *Destiny*, where the Labour candidate argues that since he is standing for election as a legislator, he is committed to believing in the validity of the laws and in the wrongness of breaking them. The sympathy of the play is with the man who equates this attitude with 'Defending our traditions. Preserve our way of life. Put Britain first. Wogs begin at Calais.' In *Wreckers* this question is central.

The first half of the play, set in 1972, concentrates on the imprisonment of five dockers under the Industrial Relations Act, interweaving their story with one about shady activities which are carried on with impunity in the rag trade. The second half moves the characters forward to 1976, when they are involved in an extremist takeover of a constituency Labour Party after the MP has declared his support for the rule of law and the imprisonment of the dockers who have defied it. The argument of the first half is that a character, Hudi, who steals, beats up his woman, and tries to drive his lorry through a picket line is no worse than the dishonest businessman—the implication being that all businessmen are dishonest. In the second half Hudi emerges as the more radical of two candidates for the position of branch secretary in the constituency. Unconcerned with whether a stretch of imprisonment has changed him in any way, David Edgar uses Hudi in an argument with the MP, weighting it so that the politician is exposed as a moderate with no sincere belief in moderation:

HUDI: That doesn't answer the question. (*Pause. Angry*) I mean, you said, the Tories couldn't give a toss, they'll break any laws you make, they'll use the House of Lords and the Stock Exchange and the bloody army, so it is kind of important to know if your precious middle ground in fact exists at all. (*Pause.*) I asked a question! (*Pause.*)
MEMBER: All right. I'll even answer it.
(*The* MEMBER *goes to the dictaphone, switches it on. We hear his* VOICE.)
VOICE: And finally, my friends, I would ask you to be realistic. We social democrats believe that in time of prosperity it is possible to remove inequality and injustice by transferring the surplus of wealth produced from the rich to the poor. But that depends on having prosperity and having a surplus. We are now having to choose—and that's what the debate on public spending is about—between social goals and the health of the wealth-making machine. Put simply, we have to choose between the interests of the needy and the interests of profitable industry. As the former depends on the latter, we really have no choice. (*He switches off the machine.*)
MEMBER: I think that means, the answer's no.

After Hudi has gone he says: 'We oppose the wreckers for many reasons. But, primarily, because, in their desire to destroy profit, they are profoundly unrealistic.' And in both halves much of the dialogue consists of jokes at the expense of the middle and upper classes, jokes which (in Griffiths's phrase) 'feed prejudice and fear and blinkered vision'.

David Hare's play *Teeth 'n' Smiles* is about a different kind of wrecking. The lead singer in a touring rock group, having lost what faith she had in pop culture as a protest movement, is drinking so much that she is liable to sabotage the show by insulting the audience. In the second set at a

Cambridge May Ball, the band starts an aggressive rock number but stops when she fails to come in on her musical cue. Instead of singing she speaks:

Now listen, kids, call you kids, so far you're schlebs and secret assholes. What you say, sir? (*She listens.*) Yeah, well, what you do with it is your business. Just don't ask me to hang it in my larder. Now this is meant to be a freak-out not a Jewish funeral. Let me make this plain. I don't play to dead yids. What you say, what are you saying, madam? (*She leans forward, her hand in front of her eyes.*) Sure. If that's what you want. Meet you in the library in half an hour. Bring your knickers in your handbag. (*She leans forward again.*) I am what? What is that word? I have not heard it before. What is stoned? (*She holds up the whisky bottle.*) This is a depressant, I take it to get depressed.

She then tries to remove the jeans from the boy playing the electric organ.

The action occurs in 1969—the year after the French students' rebellion, the beginning of the last summer in a decade that had started more promisingly. As Maggie puts it, 'The acid dream is over lezzava good time.' Some of David Hare's hatred for the Cambridge ethos is filtered through Arthur, who had been reading Music at Jesus College. David Hare had chosen Jesus because he wanted to study literature under a Marxist don, Raymond Williams; Arthur, once he got to know Maggie, had decided it would be 'academic' to go on studying. Undergraduates, he says, are 'Narcissists. . . Intellectuals. Rich complacent self-loving self-regarding self-righteous phoney half-baked politically immature neurotic evil-minded little shits.' He compares the college porter, who caught him making love to Maggie, with a German 'stormfuhrer' (*sic*) and the Cambridge academic institution—like Buchenwald in *Comedians*—is discussed as if it were a representative part of the capitalist 'system':

And everyone told me: don't waste your energy. Because that's what they want. They invent a few rules that don't mean anything so that you can ruin your health trying to change them. Then overnight they redraft them because they didn't really matter in the first place. One day it's a revolution to say fuck on the bus. Next day it's the only way to get a ticket. That's how the system works. An obstacle course.

Who are 'they'? The dons who sit on the Cambridge Senate? An international conspiracy of capitalistic oppressors? Like National Front policy-makers, this kind of play bases its appeal on giving the audience a chance to believe that there is a common enemy which can be fought.

David Hare remembers the mutual antipathy that arose between undergraduates and touring rock groups, but he dramatizes only one side of it. A great deal of space is given, very amusingly, to the contempt that the musicians feel towards their privileged audience. But the only under-graduate to be featured in the action is a medical student who does not intend to drop out until he has his degree, but claims to hate the 'system' as much as Arthur does:

ARTHUR: Still the same shit-hole, eh?
ANSON: I don't like it very much.
ARTHUR: The people don't seem to have changed.
ANSON: Oh, I don't know. There are a few more totallys, you know. I should think. I share digs with a totally. I mean, I call him a totally, what happens is he has his friends to tea, I never stay, I just occasionally have to let them in the door and I overhear them, they're always sitting there saying, 'The whole system's totally corrupt an's gotta be totally replaced by a totally new system', so I just stand at the door and say, 'Couple more totallys for you, Tom.'

In performance at the Royal Court the play made con-siderable impact. Loaded as it is with invective, the dialogue was abrasively and sometimes explosively funny. As in the creation of Jimmy Porter, enormous creative energy had been poured into the self-destructive desperation of highly articulate characters. The group will be disbanded; Maggie, like Archie Rice, will probably go to prison. In both plays the situation of the disintegrating performers is offered as a paradigm for the state of England. Archie Rice refuses to emigrate to a country where there may be no draught Bass. The final scene in *Teeth 'n' Smiles* contains a speech about a bomb falling on a ballroom designed as a replica of the ballroom on the *Titanic*; the closing lyric 'Last orders on the *Titanic*', is about letting the women and children drown. 'Man we've gotta save the crew.' Unlike Osborne, Hare spreads his desperation, his invective and his articu-lacy among several characters, but whereas Osborne identi-

fied very strongly with Jimmy and Archie, Hare feels little
warmth for anyone but Maggie and Arthur, who occupy
only a small proportion of the talking space. Though they
are made to seem more likeable than the offstage undergraduates, the musicians forfeit sympathy when they let
Maggie (who has not been taking drugs) go to prison because they have been keeping their drugs in her suitcase.
But the main blame falls on the college authorities, represented, rather inadequately, by the servile porter, Mr. Snead,
who calls in the police. An Alsatian and a uniformed
policeman appear in the tableau that ends the first act,
visually linking university discipline with police methods.

Though the play's impacts, moment by moment, were
enormous, they failed to live on in the mind. Its main de-
bility is that nearly all its ejaculations are premature. Tension is generated when the musicians, who are ninety minutes late, refuse to hurry, and by the possibility that Maggie
will be too drunk to perform. She makes her first entrance,
prostrate, carried over the shoulder of the grim college porter. The bass guitarist gives himself a fix on stage and starts
hallucinating. In performance the musicians reveal an at-
tacking energy which is quite at odds with their laconic
conversation. Maggie—a very well-written character—ironically parades her self-disgust in an interview with the
medical student, saying what she has said already in a
dozen other interviews, but casually seducing him:

MAGGIE: I only sleep with very stupid men. Write this down.
The reason I sleep with stupid men is: they never understand a word
I say. That makes me trust them.

So each one gets told a different secret, some terrible piece of my
life that only they will know. Some separate . . . awfulness. But they
don't know the rest, so they can't understand. Then the day I die,
every man I've known will make for Wembley Stadium. And each in
turn will recount his special bit. And when they are joined, they will
lighten up the sky. (*She picks up the dress* LAURA *has laid out.*)
Come on, kid, I'll change after. No point in getting another dress
dirty.

ANSON: No. (*She leads* ANSON *out.*)

The group's cynical manager, Saraffian, arrives, stealing
chicken and champagne in case they don't get paid, and

hinting at his intention of sacking Maggie, who reappears, distressed that Anson became so emotional before trying to make love to her and that he failed so abjectly. With her insulting speech to the audience and the appearance of the policeman, the first act ends very tensely, and, halfway through the second, there is another effective climax when she sets fire to the dinner tent. But the impetus is running out before the end of the act. Instead of a climax for it we get a long speech from Saraffian, describing how, as a boy from Tottenham, he was taken by a posh girl-friend to the Café de Paris on the night it was bombed. The well-turned sentences give a vivid account of the abrupt transformation:

A man lights a match and I can see that my girl-friend's clothes have been completely blown off by the blast. She is twenty-one and her champagne is now covered in a grey dust. A man is staring at his mother whose head is almost totally severed. Another man is trying to wash the wounded, he is pouring champagne over the raw stump of a girl's thigh to soothe her. Then somebody yells put the match out, we'll die if there's gas about, and indeed there was a smell, a yellow smell.

But the speech has no adequate dramatic function. It is included because David Hare wants to make a point about the class war. When Saraffian sees two men looting the dead, his first thought is 'I'm with you pal'. The speech ends, 'There is a war going on. All the time. A war of attrition.'

But this is not the point that David Hare wants to make. Maggie rejects it:

Well, I'm sure it gives you comfort, your nice little class war. It ties things up very nicely, of course, from the outside you look like any other clapped-out businessman, but inside, oh, inside you got it all worked out. (*Pause.*) This man has believed the same thing for thirty years. And it does not show. Is that going to happen to us? Fucking hell, somebody's got to keep on the move.

David Hare has said that *Teeth 'n' Smiles* is about 'whether we have any chance of changing ourselves';[19] the prognosis is negative. Superficially the play may have little resemblance to his other 1975 play, *Fanshen*, a dramatization of

19 Interview in *Theatre Quarterly*, nos. 19–20.

William Hinton's book about the Chinese revolution. But in both works the fundamental concern is with the possibility of change. In China the political, social, economic, and cultural conditions made it possible; here they do not.

ARTHUR: I knew a guy, played in a band. They were loud, they were very loud. What I mean by loud is: they made Pink Floyd sound like a Mozart quintet. I said to him, why the hell don't you wear muffs? In eighteen months you're going to be stone deaf. He said: that's why we play so loud. The louder we play, the sooner we won't be able to hear. I can see us all. Rolling down the highway into middle age. Complacency. Prurience. Sadism. Despair.
(SARAFFIAN *gets out a hip flask*.)
SARAFFIAN: Don't worry. Have some brandy.

If *Teeth 'n' Smiles* survives, it will be because it is vivid, forceful, moving, and funny in the account it gives of desperation and self-destructiveness in a group of youngsters, not because it succeeds in establishing that group as representative of young people at the end of the Sixties or because of the revolutionary message it implies. In common with David Hare, Stephen Poliakoff has not only a disturbing talent for portraying self-destructiveness, but also a tendency to embed socio-political generalizations in dramatic action. *Clever Soldiers* (produced 1974) resembles *Teeth 'n' Smiles* in its uncompromising indictment of privileged education. Set just before and just after the outbreak of the First World War, *Clever Soldiers* shows how a popular, good-looking public schoolboy, Teddy, habitually as condescending to fans as to fags, becomes an Oxford undergraduate and later an officer who chews quizzically on the cud of other people's subservience. Why should they do what he tells them?

The structural argument is that sixty years of social change have failed to alter the function of public school and university, which is to inculcate a sense of superiority. And we are shown how this can snap and cut back into self-destructiveness. Teddy is appalled to find himself emulating the behaviour of the brother officers who make the fighting into a sport—'Let's get to their touchline'—without placing any value on the non-commissioned lives they are risking, and equally appalled at the unquestioning obedience of the men, even when aware of their leaders' inadequacy. To punish himself he goads a private soldier into beating him up.

Poliakoff was only twenty-one when he wrote the play, and lacking in technical *savoir-faire*, but he achieved remarkable intensity. The dialogue crackles with nervous electricity, and the climax of self-destructive violence—as when a girl chews a razor blade and Teddy follows suit—emerge not merely as isolated outcrops of theatricality. The tension may emanate from guilt feelings about social and educational privilege, but Poliakoff instinctively knows how to exploit this atmospherically. The opening public-school scene mingles complacent social superiority with latent homosexuality. In the first Oxford sequence, the theme of class war is introduced through a working-class don, David, who talks rather implausibly about his humble Welsh background and the 'magnificent hatred' he feels towards Oxford. He is contrasted, somewhat schematically, with Teddy's room-mate, Harold, a homosexual aesthete, perhaps loosely modelled on Harold Acton. Through a girl with whom Teddy has an affair, the theme of Women's Lib is anachronistically introduced. Altogether there is little sense of period.

David primes Teddy to regard the war as a kind of dress-rehearsal for the world revolution which must ensue, and when Teddy enlists, David presents him with a Dostoevsky novel. Poliakoff's central characters are themselves Dostoevskyan in their lust for a purity they can achieve only through action prompted largely by self-hatred. Poliakoff himself seems sensually attracted to the idea of world revolution at the same time as fearing it. He makes David say:

Very soon there's going to be such a holocaust you know. The world's biggest battle, bigger than anything ever before, and whatever the outcome, this revulsion is going to start working. This wave of revulsion—and revenge, that is building all the time, is going to reach explosive proportions, and will sweep the country, see, and it'll be of such intensity, such sheer colossal size, that it's going to penetrate the minds of every little bastard in this country. Each one... even the most sluggish—the most deceived, even the totally passive. It's going to completely slash through this stupor we're in—do you hear, boy, and everything will go down before it. This government, this place, and all its assorted barbarizing, the whole hierarchy will collapse. Smashed clean open, stunned out of existence. Nobody . . .that was responsible for all this can possibly survive it. It can't. That's certain and inevitable. The war has only lasted as long as it has, because of the strength of what it's removing. But you can feel it already—the force of what's coming, for the natural thing is going to happen, boy.

But if Poliakoff partly relishes the idea of being destroyed, he at least succeeds in projecting the feeling into Teddy's scene with the private. After provoking the man into hitting him, Teddy threatens him with a court-martial, orders him to shoot him, and, when the private refuses, strikes him across the face. The play ends, aptly, back at Oxford, where very little has changed.

Heroes (produced 1975) is another play about fascism. Set ambiguously in a big city, which might be either German or British, at a time which might be either the Twenties or the Eighties, it ends with the two 'heroes' astride a motorcycle which will take them to the Party headquarters, where they will commit themselves to joining. Despite the refusal to specify, Poliakoff succeeds very well in evoking the atmosphere of the place, conveying strong impressions of desperation and growing militancy among the unemployed, with children taking to prostitution and the government failing to control the spread of armed violence. Like Brenton, Poliakoff gives us sharply disturbing glimpses of what Britain could become if democracy is eroded and if inflation and unemployment get out of control. Howard Nemerov once said that the writer's gift of prophecy 'is not to invent the world that will be there in the future but to bring into being the mind that will be there in the future'. Brenton, Barker, and Poliakoff all act on the opposite principle. Though Poliakoff's tone is less admonitory than Brenton's or Barker's, all three depict the mentality they would like to abort.

In comparison with *The Churchill Play* and *That Good Between Us, Heroes* is remarkably free from the tendency to categorize characters into good and bad. In fact the two 'heroes', Julius and Rainer, look rather like representatives of the aristocrat and the prole, and, as in *Clever Soldiers*, the hysterical self-destructiveness in the aristocrat provides some of the most theatrical moments—as when Julius removes the bulb from a lamp in order to pep himself up with electric shocks, or when he goes almost berserk with a pair of cymbals.

His relationship with Rainer is not consistently plausible, though it gets off to a very good start when the scruffy, disgruntled workman bursts into the room where the young dandy is still pleasurably abed quite late in the morning. The intruder starts rummaging through the drawers and threatening to take possession of the room, ignoring Julius's polite protests. If a man has never worked, except as a dilettante artist, living on a private income, what right does he have to his possessions?

Poliakoff's writing is at its best when violence is impending. The offstage noises of the stormy Communist demonstration are reminiscent of a sequence in *Clever Soldiers* when Teddy and his girl-friend are listening nervously to the offstage noises of the marauding 'bloods', liable to smash up people's rooms. In *Heroes* the sequence of throwing stones to smash the police searchlight is also highly effective. The weakness of the play is that the plot depends heavily on the developing relationship between the two men, a relationship which is written only very sketchily.

There is one café scene in which the characters are paying inflationary prices for insipid, rubbishy cakes, which they angrily denounce. In Poliakoff's other 1975 play, *Hitting Town*, there is a similar scene in a Leicester Wimpy bar, where the incestuous brother and sister, enraged at waiting so long for service, concoct an uneatable meal out of condiments, finally cutting open a plastic tomato to discover, floating in the ketchup, a tooth, half a sardine, chewing gum and cigarette ends. The consummation of the incestuous relationship is less effective than the build-up to it, and the character of the sister, oscillating between complicity and shocked reticence, is not so well written as that of the tense, charming, cynical, reckless boy, irritably turning his aggression inwards in order to fight his way out of boredom and mediocrity. He is a more plausible, more deeply thought-out character than Teddy in *Clever Soldiers*. The dialogue thrusts embarrassingly at the audience's threshold of propriety. A sequence involving a handful of dead beetles is particularly skin-erupty (to use D. H. Lawrence's word for Strindberg) and there is an amusing sequence introducing the bland voice of a disc jockey on a local radio phone-in. He reacts with puritanical intolerance, sharpened to please his listeners, when Ralph rings in provocatively, pretending to be a boy of eleven who is having sex with his sister.

The disc jockey, Leonard Brazil, becomes the main character in the companion play, *City Sugar* (produced 1976), which is less frantic, more controlled, more resonant, subtler in characterization. The action is again set in Leicester and Nicola, the girl who had been working in the Wimpy bar, reappears as a supermarket salesgirl. Leonard is also on the point of changing jobs. An ex-teacher, he despises himself for pumping unstimulating trash into the young minds he is no longer trying to educate, but he cannot resist the lure of a lucrative job with a commercial radio company in London. Towards the audience which laps up the footling wisecracks he energetically pours out he feels more contempt than compassion, but his other relationships are ambivalent. He seems to dislike the studio assistant, who not only gawps at him adoringly but copies him shrewdly, grooming himself to follow on in the job, and, when the moment comes, Leonard helps him. Hearing the flat voice of Nicola over the telephone, he knows she represents the median type of the girls who form his public; he also feels sexually attracted to her, as the studio assistant guesses.

The meeting with Nicola is cleverly delayed as Poliakoff cuts between the studio, the supermarket, and the bedsitter, where she stuffs almost everything she owns into a life-size doll, a floppy replica of a pop star. She is making it for a competition devised by Leonard, who rigs the results to make her one of the finalists, and the confrontation between them in the studio is effectively anti-climactic.

They are disappointed in each other, unable to communicate, unwilling to try. In a long-delayed outburst of hysteria
she flings a plastic cup of milk—another image linking
nourishment with artificiality—on the floor, and in the
middle of the live transmission (a quiz competition with
one other finalist) she tries to walk out of the studio. Mostly,
though, the tension is kept under control until Leonard
manipulates both girls into humiliating races around the
control panel in a game of swapping chairs. Like Teddy in
Clever Soldiers, he is more appalled than pleased at other
people's willingness to do what he tells them.

There was a touch of revenge, don't you think? I must want a little
revenge. . . . I glanced at you before the last question and saw that
stare, that blank, infuriatingly vacant gaze, and then it just happened.
I wanted to see just how far I *could push you*, how much you'd
take—I was hoping you'd come back—that something would come
shooting back, that you'd put up a fight, Nicola. That you'd explode,
Nicola, you'd explode. Do you see, why didn't you why don't you?
What's the matter with all you kids now, what is it?

Afterwards, when he reverts to his schoolmaster persona,
trying to exert power through patronizing advice, she defends herself with sulky silence. Going back to her supermarket, she considers the possibility of wrecking it, but decides
not to.

Leonard's final speech to his radio audience strikes the
same note as the final sequence in *Teeth 'n' Smiles*, ironically suggesting that the best of the options still open is
distraction from reality:

I'll be giving a few jokes and all the hits and more, all the sounds and
more, all the luck and more, where I'll be seeing us through our
present troubles, obliterating the bad times—that's a Big Word—and
remembering the good times, oh yes, and letting people remember
and letting them forget. Drowning all our sorrows, yes I said drowning, till we're emerging out of the clouds, of course. . . .

We're going to lick it, of course we will. No need to worry, no
need to be sad. Shout that out. So tune in, I said tune in. Because I'll
take your minds off things, oh yes, I will. (*He brings the music in
louder.*)

Mixing mimicry with parody, this reproduction of disc-
jockey language brings Leonard's self-contempt into focus,
but not his self-pity or his self-indulgence.

Poliakoff's *Strawberry Fields* (produced 1977) is another play about fascism in Britain today, but instead of focusing on the National Front, he takes two imaginary extremists, a girl and a boy. The two acts each end with a shooting, and this points to the play's main flaw. Both *coups de théâtre* are facile alternatives to conclusions that could have been reached only if the writing had penetrated more deeply into its subject matter. The girl, Charlotte, is characterized as ecologically a conservationist and politically an ultra-conservative. She carries a revolver, which she uses to shoot a policeman who wants to search her while she is travelling about the country, distributing pamphlets, accompanied by a boy who thinks he is going blind. Both of them seem to be verging on madness, but, since Poliakoff, like the other political playwrights, is adamantly averse to dramatic analysis in terms of individual psychology, the paranoia remains out of focus. The action proceeds as an episodic adventure story as they move about from place to place, meeting potential sympathizers in the first act (which is sometimes reminiscent of *Destiny*) and on the run from the police in the second. In both acts Poliakoff repeats some of the effects he has pulled off more crisply in other plays, and he is less at home with a plot that involves movement from one locale to another. Feeling trapped as he does in a social situation he hates, he is best at brewing up the kind of theatrical atmosphere that suggests a claustrophobic oppressiveness, whether in a city like Leicester or in a nameless metropolis like the one in *Heroes*.

His television play *Stronger than the Sun* (transmitted 1977) suffers similarly from his refusal to treat character in psychological terms. Again the principal initiatives are taken by a fanatical girl, but this time she is a radical. She works in a plant where imported plutonium waste is processed in pressured water reactors, and she is convinced that the government's nuclear policy is based on wilful underestimation of the dangers. She decides to help the campaign for gas-cooled reactors (which are safer) by smuggling a small quantity of plutonium out of the plant to demonstrate publicly that the security arrangements are inadequate. She succeeds in the smuggling, but fails to get any publicity either from the pressure group which is campaigning for an alternative nuclear policy or from the *Sunday Times* journalist she had expected to be interested. Her ultra-nervous behaviour in the pub meeting with him, and her subsequent attempt to get her own publicity by using the stolen plutonium in a suicide attempt make her seem insane, but, as with the girl in *Strawberry Fields*, Poliakoff sidesteps all problems of personality. Though it could be argued, in both cases, that social and political pressures have fomented the tendency to behave unreasonably, it is individual behaviour that drama pushes into the foreground. To abstain from psychological analysis is to leave the foreground unfocused.

None of these nine playwrights would be interested in telling a story without social significance. Perhaps there is no such thing as a story that does not illustrate a social process, but from Sophocles onwards playwrights have devised different means of interweaving public and private themes. Long before the present wave of political drama, they had evolved an extensive repertoire of techniques by which a character could be set up as representative of a nation, a type, a generation, a group, or a class. But the medium tends to insist on single combat as a means of settling disputes, and the more theatrical a confrontation is, the more it individualizes the combatants. Antigone is not merely a representative of private conscience, Creon not merely an incarnation of the social superego. Brecht's Puntila is no more a typical employer than Matti is a typical servant. Not that there is any such phenomenon as a typical boss or a typical worker; the anti-bourgeois stereotypes of Marxist drama may be no worse than the comic housemaids of drawing-room comedy, but they are no better.

In all drama, characterization is liable to be determined partly by the need for contrast. Goneril and Regan must be unlike Cordelia, Macduff the anti-type of Macbeth. But the writer is more limited both in planning and in developing his contrasts if each character is conceived as representative of a group, and if the purpose of the play is to reassert predetermined ideas about conflict between the groups. 'Drama as literature', wrote Gerhart Hauptmann in 1912, 'is not so much the ready-made result of thought as the thinking process itself.' The process can be directed at social themes, as it is in many of Ibsen's and Chekhov's best plays, but these always give the impression of an openmindedness that has survived into the act of writing. The characters are never condemned before they are brought to life, like the middle-class characters in plays by Arden and D'Arcy, McGrath, Bond, Brenton, and Barker. It would be unthinkable for a landowner in Bond or a Cabinet minister in Barker to be allowed any dialogue or any behaviour that might engage sympathy. Nor is this facile contrast between working-class heroes and middle-class villains the only simplification that occurs in contemporary political plays. Very often dramatized argument and analysis give way to entertaining but implausible violence in melodramatic climaxes, the underlying sentimentality being disguised by brutality. Catering for Victorian audiences, melodramatists coated the moralistic pill with sugar; contemporary melodramatists use viciousness. The *coups de théâtre* in the work of Bond, Brenton, Barker, and Poliakoff are undeniably effective, but the recourse to violent killing serves almost every time as an alternative to continuing the thinking process.

Dutiful commitment to an ideology is likely to interfere with the artistic duty of developing the material's narrative potential. In *The Bundle, The Churchill Play*, and *Destiny*, for instance, action and characterization are visibly cramped or even deformed by exigencies of pattern and argument, as if the writers had operated in the way Margaretta D'Arcy likes to operate, thinking of a subject 'that requires to be dramatized', and only then finding 'a story to embody the theme' and 'a style to narrate the story'. Some of these plays are less journalistic and ephemeral than others, but there is a tendency for drama to gravitate in the direction of television and journalism. The stage playwright is now forced to offer something that will draw at least some people away from the free entertainment available every evening on television. But it can be disastrous to let the television play serve as a model for the stage play. David Edgar's *Wreckers* and Brenton's *The Churchill Play* might both have been better written if they had been designed to be more durable.

The other great danger of political orientation is that it blinkers the playwright's vision. Kenneth Tynan once wrote: 'There is today hardly an aspect of human suffering (outside the realm of medicine) for which politics, psychiatry and environmental psychology cannot offer at least a *tentative* solution.'[20] To write a play as if this were true is to dismiss all such experimental attempts as Beckett and Ionesco have made to characterize the human condition. Political playwrights tend to ignore such subjects as sexual jealousy, the frustrations of marriage, the agonies of divorce, ugliness, friendship, betrayal, and a sense of personal inadequacy, to concentrate systematically on problems that might be remedied by social reform or revolution. *The Cherry Orchard* centres on a decadent class's inability to adjust to social change, but what brings the action so richly to life is Chekhov's ability to identify sympathetically with a variety of viewpoints quite unlike his own, and to construct a comic theatrical mosaic out of the suffering that has resulted from the frustration of the characters' objectives. Politics, psychiatry, and environmental psychology could not provide much help for Ranyevskaya, Gaev, Trofimov, Lopakhin, or Epihodov. It is not because this is a pre-revolutionary society that the people fail to master their weaknesses, that a girl prefers a man who doesn't want her to another who does, that a woman falls prey to a parasitic lover and goes on giving away money she can't afford to everyone who asks, that an ageing bachelor uncle tries to impress his young nieces by making promises he can't fulfil. Revolution can do nothing to stop people from feeling they have missed most of their best opportunities,

[20] *Tynan Right and Left*, p. 67.

and usually they are right. Some of the plays I have been discussing—*Teeth 'n' Smiles* and *City Sugar*, for instance—are enriched with humour and with compassionate observation of suffering and self-contempt, but most of them are lacking in humour and willingness to empathize with characters the writer sets up to represent enemies in the class war.

4 New relationships

In the British theatre of today there is less occasion for using the words experimental or *avant-garde* than at any other time since the war. In the late Forties we had the Arts Theatre, the Mercury, the Embassy, the Watergate, and several other small theatres, where low-budget productions of poetic drama and experimental plays by unknown writers could be tried out. Sunday-night productions without décor began at the Royal Court in 1957, and this is how the theatre launched Arnold Wesker's *The Kitchen* and work by Alun Owen, Wole Soyinka, Gwyn Thomas, Edward Bond, David Cregan, Heathcote Williams, and Howard Brenton. In 1968 Jim Haynes, who had founded the small Traverse Theatre in Edinburgh five years earlier, opened an Arts Lab in Drury Lane. It not only gave hospitality to some of the earliest fringe groups, including the People Show (which had been started in 1966 by Jeff Nuttall), it brought others into existence. Pip Simmons formed a company to put on a series of 50-minute plays at the Arts Lab, while David Hare and Tony Bicat, who were later to form Portable Theatre, collaborated to compile a show out of Kafka's Diaries.

The demise of the Arts Lab in 1969 was as catalytic as its existence had been. Pip Simmons had to find other venues, while David Hare and Tony Bicat wanted to take their productions into a variety of non-theatrical contexts. So, in the same way that sixteenth-century groups of touring players built up a circuit of towns they could successfully revisit, a new network of regional bases was created, mostly in university towns, some on campus, some outside it. With over 40 universities, most of them new, England now had a very large student population, spread all over the country, and it formed the basis of the new audience. Many of the fringe groups took to touring, and non-fringe groups like the RSC's Theatregoround and Prospect Theatre Company—both directed by university graduates—started to visit the same places.

Playing in buildings which had not been designed as theatres, to audiences that were accustomed to television but not to live theatrical entertainment, and moving about from place to place with no hope of building up either a regular public or the kind of style that depends on familiarity, the actors had to buttonhole the audience, and the writers had recourse to shock tactics and unsophisticated comedy. Unlike the Elizabethan audience, which could concentrate on long speeches because it was in the habit of using its ears to follow speeches, sermons, church services and ballads, the provincial audience of the Sixties was habituated to taking in information mainly through its eyes. This encouraged playwrights and directors to depend on physical means of expression, and this tendency coincided with a reaction against the tradition of English acting that centred more on the Voice Beautiful than on the body. 'You must have plays with a strong physical force,' David Hare said. 'You have to find the lowest common denominator for a show.' In their first production, the Kafka adaptation, he says, 'We bashed and bashed our audiences with a long steady stream of neurosis.'[1] And he has said: 'The idea was to take theatre to places where it normally didn't go. We weren't to see that a variety of arts centres and groups would spring up to accommodate that. But when we started we played more army camps and bare floors than we were playing by the end.'[2]

It had been obvious since the end of the war that theatre could not survive healthily without appealing to a wider stratum of the public. During the war 'Art for the People' had been not merely an ideal. Founded in December 1939 to boost public morale, the Council for the Encouragement

[1] Interview with Peter Ansorge, *Plays and Players*, op. cit.
[2] Interview in *Theatre Quarterly*, nos. 19–20.

of Music and the Arts had considerable success with its theatrical tours, and in 1945, when the Council was reconstituted as the Arts Council, under the same chairman, the economist John Maynard Keynes, he defined its objective (in a speech on the radio) as: 'to create an environment, to breed a spirit, to cultivate an opinion, to offer a stimulus to such purpose that the artist and the public can each sustain and live on the other in that union which has occasionally existed in the past at the great ages of a communal civilized life.' Since the Middle Ages the only period of English theatrical history which can be called great in this sense is the Shakespearian period, when productions which depended more on the spoken word than on spectacle had a strong, immediate appeal to an audience representative of all social classes. It was Keynes's theory that the greatness of the Elizabethan theatre could be explained in economic terms:

We were just in a financial position to afford Shakespeare at the moment when he presented himself . . . by far the larger proportion of the world's great writers and artists have flourished in the atmosphere of buoyancy, exhilaration and the freedom from economic cares felt by the governing class, which is engendered by profit inflations.[3]

But Arts Council subsidy was of little help to Joan Littlewood, who made a most strenuous and serious attempt to create a theatre for the people. In 1945 she formed her Theatre Workshop, and in 1953 she moved it into the Theatre Royal, Stratford East; but though her inclinations were anti-literary and her productions drew robustly on the techniques of popular theatre, she was unable to attract the East End audience she wanted. Her public was not very different from the public that patronized West End theatres, and the most successful of her shows transferred to the West End. She was working-class by birth and anti-intellectual by disposition; paradoxically, it was writers and directors of middle-class origin and university education who were to take more successful initiatives in persuading a

[3] *A Treatise on Money* (1930), vol. II, p. 174.

working-class audience into theatre-going habits—Jim Haynes; Michael Kustow and Terry Hands of the RSC, who made a success of Theatregoround; David Hare and Tony Bicat of Portable.

But why hasn't the healthy growth of fringe theatre led to a healthy development of experimental theatre? A movement needs a centre, and the main characteristic of the fringe is diffusion, the main currents in its activity centrifugal. John Arden and John McGrath are the two most obvious examples of talented writers who have rejected London in favour of a close relationship with local audiences in the regions. We have no Fringe Festival in England, and nothing comparable to the annual Experimenta at Frankfurt, which played an important part in encouraging and publicizing the emergence of several young playwrights including Peter Handke. Nor is there now anything comparable to the Royal Court Theatre as it was in the late Fifties and early Sixties with its Sunday night productions. Until the middle Sixties, it looked as though the Royal Shakespeare Company might be taking over from the Royal Court the responsibility of encouraging experiment. This was due mainly to Peter Brook, who in 1962, when invited to become a director of the RSC, accepted on condition that the company should subsidize experimental work to be carried on separately from the Stratford and Aldwych seasons. During its experimental season at the Arts Theatre in 1962, the company produced plays by Rudkin, Boris Vian, Giles Cooper, Henry Livings, and Fred Watson, together with plays by Gorky and Middleton; there was the experimental *Theatre of Cruelty* season at the LAMDA Theatre in 1964 and a programme at the Aldwych featuring work by Beckett, Arrabal, Whiting, James Saunders, and Jean Tardieu under the title *Expeditions One. Expeditions Two* followed in 1965 with work by Charles Wood, Johnny Speight, Irene Coates, and David Mercer. But the series ended there, and no one could apply the word 'experimental' to the RSC's 1971 season at The Place, with work by Strindberg, Robert Montgomery, and Trevor Griffiths, or to the 1977—8 season at the Warehouse, with work by

Shakespeare, Brecht, Bond, C. P. Taylor, Howard Barker, James Robson, and Barrie Keeffe.

That we have no intelligent theatre magazine is another symptom of the present malaise. From the middle of the Fifties till the middle of the Sixties, the commentaries in *Encore* were influential in focusing and encouraging enthusiasm for the work of playwrights (including Whiting and Arden) who needed nurturing.

Without experimental writing a theatre cannot be altogether healthy, but is the English theatre to be judged entirely by its playwrights? Since 1955 a great deal has changed radically. At last we have a National Theatre and another national company with bases in London and Stratford. And after nearly fifty years (1910–57) in which hardly any theatres were constructed, millions of pounds have been spent on new buildings, where production is no longer cramped by the shapes and rigidities that were dictated during the Victorian and Edwardian periods by the relationship needed then between acting area and auditorium. The phrase 'fourth wall' dates back to the beginning of the nineteenth century, when Leigh Hunt used it in describing the actor John Bannister: 'The stage appears to be his own room, of which the audience compose the fourth wall.' This was illusionist theatre, the other three walls forming a three-dimensional picture in which the actor moved, his face made up to benefit from coloured spotlights and footlights, which, together with the proscenium arch, created a Rubicon to exclude the audience from the world of moving pictures. No sign was ever given that actors or characters were aware of the audience's presence. In the post-Brechtian, anti-illusionist theatre of today, attention is repeatedly drawn to the fact that the performance is a living artefact, and the whole relationship between actor and audience is much more fluid. Make-up and coloured illumination count for less. Acting style has become less rhetorical. The modern actor does not want to dominate or to enchant his public, and he is less dependent

than his pre-war predecessor on charm. There is less form-
ality, less illusion, less inequality, and more rapport in the
relationship between actor and audience.

The change is radical, and it is puzzling that playwrights
have not taken more advantage of it. To the extent that
the scenic element has become less important and the verbal element more important, the development is in the
writer's favour, but in the constant triangular power
struggle between writer, director and actor, it is the director
who has gained most. Artaud wanted the director to become the true author of the dramatic event, taking responsibility both for all the non-verbal elements in the production
and for the way text was spoken. Generally, words have
become less important, partly because of the widespread
loss of faith in language. Artaud's influence has played its
part, together with successive waves of anti-literary, anti-
cultural, anti-verbal feeling. Songs have encroached further
and further into 'legitimate' theatre, while dance, mime,
gesture, posture, movement, and improvisation have bulked
larger. So has silence. Drama schools devote more time to
the actor's body, less to his voice; it can no longer be said
of English actors that they are dead below the neck.

The devaluation of the word has increased the importance of the director. Working with existing scripts, he can
take the initiative in exploiting the new theatrical spaces
and shapes, and he can develop the possibilities of the new
relationship between performers and public. He can also
do what Hauptmann thought only the writer could do: use
theatre as a means of thinking. One of the earliest attempts
to do this was made in Joan Littlewood's production of
Oh What a Lovely War, though it may never become clear
how credit should be apportioned either for the concept or
for the text. The playwright Ted Allan claims that he wrote
it, but that Joan Littlewood 'threw out my main plot, kept
my peripheral scenes, rewriting most of them, took my
name off the play in England, and gave writing credits to a
few hundred people, to indicate that nobody *wrote* it.'[4] It

[4] Statement in *Contemporary Dramatists*, op. cit., p. 30.

has also been said that Gerry Raffles, the general manager of the company, conceived the idea after hearing a Black and White Minstrel Show devoted to songs of the First World War. The only authorial credits on the programme were to Charles Chilton and the company. Charles Chilton, an expert on music hall, may have suggested more than how the songs could be used, and many of the best ideas derived, no doubt, from the actors, individually and collectively, in improvisation. Ted Allan is not the only playwright to complain that Joan Littlewood interfered with his script, and for each one who spoke out against her, there must have been ten who preserved a decorous but resentful silence. Justified though the resentment is, she must be recognized as the great pioneer of the growing collaborative flexibility we now enjoy. In the early Sixties she was the only important director in England to allow actors to contribute creatively to a text. As she said,

I do not believe in the supremacy of the director, designer, actor or even the writer. It is through collaboration that this knockabout art of theatre survives and kicks. . . . No one mind or imagination can foresee what a play will become until all the physical and intellectual stimuli which are crystallized in the poetry of the author, have been understood by a company, and then tried out in terms of mime, discussion and the precise music of grammar; words and movement allied and integrated.[5]

But it is the director who must engineer the collective understanding and organize the integration by orchestrating the contributions the actors each make. A production consists of a series of impacts which induce a series of mood-changes. If *Oh What a Lovely War* expressed an attitude to the First World War, it was because Joan Littlewood had, in effect, used the actors, the songs, and the words to reconsider the historical events. Rehearsal as collective thought-process, piloted by the director; show as conclusion, always tentative, emphasis and internal balance varying from night to night.

The more the actor contributes—conceptually, verbally,

---

[5] Statement quoted by Charles Marowitz in a review in *Encore*, reprinted in *Confessions of a Counterfeit Critic* (1973), p. 65.

and physically—the more need there is for co-ordination from the director, who is pushed towards the role that Artaud prescribed for him as true author of the dramatic event. So it is no accident that *Oh What a Lovely War* represents a turning point in the history of the English theatre. Joan Littlewood had long been influenced by Brecht, and in 1955, at the Devon Festival, she had played the title role in the first English production of *Mutter Courage*, which she directed herself. Eight years later, in *Oh What a Lovely War*, she achieved the first triumphant mingling of Brechtian alienation with Artaudian discontinuity.[6] Some of the songs came from the trenches, some from the music halls. Costumes bridged between pierrot shows and military uniforms, performance style oscillated between vaudeville and Living Newspaper productions of the Thirties, dialogue between gibberish and verbatim reproductions of Earl Haig's speeches. Joan Littlewood performed a miracle of integration, not by ironing out the discontinuities but by emphasizing them. The preposterousness of the stylistic mixture has been imitated so often since 1963 that it is hard to recall the impact it made then, but style was inseparable from substance in the resultant exposure of historical falsifications. Ruthlessness, mindlessness, and inefficiency had been disguised as recklessness, patriotism, and courageous disregard for actualities. In the fighting itself there had been elements of farce as well as mass slaughter; reducing the slaughter to statistics, the production focused on the anomalies. Most ingenious and most influential of all were the transitions which Joan Littlewood contrived, a series of giddying jolts as hilarity faded into pathos or solemnity was displaced by obscenity.

Charles Marowitz, in his review of the production for *Encore*, was quick to recognize its importance as an essay in discontinuity: 'No sooner has the production adopted one stance than it flips into another, but despite these endless modulations, there is no sense of contradiction. This is not merely the simplex two-dimensionalism of black

[6] See above, pp. 38–9.

comedy where laughter freezes up into menace, but the multi-dimensionalism of true Epic Theatre where styles appear in order to serve the nature of what is being said, and what is being said is constantly being varied.' For Marowitz the experience was crucial, and nothing he has done in the theatre is more important than carrying the germ of discontinuity from Joan Littlewood to Peter Brook. At the end of 1963 he began to collaborate with Brook on preparations for the *Theatre of Cruelty* season which they co-directed at the LAMDA Theatre. The preliminary work was designed to break down Stanislavskian habits based on the logic of continuity. To think in terms of 'through-lines' and 'super-objectives' is to bead sequences together on a single string of intention, phasing development along a preconceived line of character. Marowitz devised exercises and improvisations to inculcate what he called a discontinuous style of acting. For instance, two actors in mid-scene would be cut short by the entrance of a third, performing an unrelated series of actions. They would have to adapt theirs to his until all three were interrupted by a fourth, and so on.

Peter Brook had long been aware that actors do most of their best work in the rehearsal room, that repetition is a deadly enemy of creativity, that a long run—the crown of success—weighs heavily on the actor's head. During the first nineteen years of his career (1945–63) Brook was not consistently and resolutely experimental in his approach. But the 1964 season at the LAMDA Theatre formed a watershed in his development. The programme carried a note comparing the experiment to a scientific research project, and warning the audience that it was watching 'a public session of work-in-progress: improvisation, exploration, and a re-examination of accepted theatre forms'. The critics ignored the admonition, reviewing the show as if it were a finished work. Since then Brook has been more wary of exposing actors to the public before preparation has solidified into performance, but he has contrived an artificial situation in which actors can go on working as if they were rehearsing, but without the pressure of having to put on a show within a limited period. Since he founded the International Centre for Theatre Research in Paris (in 1968) he has tended to spend most of his time working with actors, experimenting, doing exercises, working on lines taken from plays, ideas taken from myths, developing expressive sounds and movements as alternatives to dialogue, approximating as closely as possible to perfecting the voice and body as performing instruments, but rarely exposing the work in public performances, and then only when it needs exposure, never for the sake of publicity or money. If all theatrical work takes place in a quadrilateral with director, actor, audience, and writer as the four points, Brook has thickened the line between director and actor at the expense of the three other lines.

Artaud wanted (as he told André Gide in a letter of 7 August 1932), to 'realize a physical and spatial poetry which has long been missing from theatre'. He spoke in his manifesto for the Theatre of Cruelty of an 'alternative natural language', a physical language which could short-circuit 'all the hiatus between mind and tongue, in which we see what might be called the impotence of language'. Like Artaud, Brook has come to believe that all thought is physical, that an actor should be able to eliminate any gap between impulse and expression. Brook wants to evolve 'a theatre language as agile and penetrating as the Elizabethans created...intensity, immediacy, and density of expression'.[7] And like Artaud, who also used the Elizabethan theatre as a point of reference, Brook argues that words can no longer perform a central function as they did four hundred years ago: 'I believe in the word in classical drama, because the word was their tool. I do not believe in the word much today, because it has outlived its purpose. Words do not communicate, they do not express much, and most of the time they fail abysmally to define.'[8] During rehearsals for the *Theatre of Cruelty* season, actors were encouraged to make sounds that had nothing to do with words, and to use

---

[7] Quoted in A. C. H. Smith, *Orghast at Persepolis* (1972), p. 16.
[8] 'Search for a Hunger', *Encore*, no. 32 (July–August 1961).

words for expression of something quite irrelevant to their normal meaning.

In his production of Peter Weiss's *Marat-Sade* later in 1964 Brook used many of the same actors and many of the same techniques for non-verbal communication. The experimental work during rehearsals was designed to culminate in a marriage between *mise en scène* and a text that already existed in its entirety. *US*, which he directed in 1966, was comparable to *Oh What a Lovely War* as an example of production as thought-process. The subject was the Vietnam war, still in progress but already being falsified by the manufacture of myth. The thought-process was aimed to penetrate beyond propaganda and the misrepresentations of newsmen and photographers. Brook worked with the actors to search improvisationally for the answer to such questions as: 'If I say I care about Vietnam, how does that influence the way I spend my time?' Some scripted material was provided by Dennis Cannan, but much of the text was invented during rehearsal.

The ambiguity of the title posed the question of how far the British should feel involved in American responsibility for the Vietnam war. In fact *US* was no less political than any of the plays discussed in the last chapter, but unlike the playwrights of the new Marxist orthodoxy Brook was not merely using the medium to put across a predetermined message. No attempt was made to offer facile solutions or to prescribe attitudes for the audience to adopt. The sequence that relied most on dialogue was about a man who had decided on a protest suicide, parallel with those of the Vietnamese Buddhist monks who were pouring petrol over themselves to die in the flames. He was seen in argument with a girl of liberal convictions who had no faith in the effectiveness of self-immolation. The scene culminated in hysteria as she screamed out her demand that the war should spread to this country. She wanted to see napalm on suburban lawns. Kenneth Tynan, who accuses Brook of 'shallow and factitious pessimism', and of being a 'pure master of the theatrical gesture', has complained that he was merely using the Vietnamese war to 'get at' the

Hampstead intellectuals,[9] but Ronald Bryden, writing in *The Observer*, argued that the production contained 'moments of brilliance which advance the theatre's frontiers historically', while in *The Times* Irving Wardle wrote that he had never experienced such a successful theatrical assault on the audience's detachment.

In 1968, when Brook started work in Paris, recruiting actors of different nationalities for his experimental workshop, he was contriving a situation that would force him to concern himself with the problem of breaking through linguistic boundaries. When he commissioned Ted Hughes to invent a new language, he was not merely showing his dissatisfaction with the degenerate English we now speak and write, he was wanting to test how far human beings could ignore differences of race, language, and cultural tradition, communicating through movements and sounds, using the lowest common multiples of human expressiveness and raising them to a higher power. As Brook asked in *The Empty Space* (1968), 'Is there another language, just as exacting for the author, as a language of words? Is there a language of actions, a language of sounds—a language of word-as-part-of-movement, or word-as-lie, word-as-parody, of word-as-rubbish, of word-as-contradiction, of word-shock or word-cry?' And can new words be minted out of sounds that will have a comprehensible meaning dependent on their sound and regardless of the different semantic connotations they might have in different countries?

Orghast was the name used both for Hughes's language and for Brook's production at Persepolis in 1971, which implied a rejection of English literature, the English theatre, and the English language. No director had ever made a more decisive gesture against his mother tongue, and the cultural traditions built up in it. This is the negative aspect of what Brook was doing; the inseparable positive is that he was trying to create a form of drama immediately comprehensible to any human being. Was it possible to traverse linguistic and cultural frontiers by forging a theatrical language

[9] *Theatre Quarterly*, no. 25 (Spring 1977).

out of sounds, newly coined words, words from archaic languages expressively inflected, integrating gesture, posture, grouping and other visual elements with the sounds? The intention was to find the answer to this question through studio experiment and performance, testing the results of the work, phase by phase, on different audiences in different places.

In the production at Persepolis some of the visual effects were spectacular. No one could have failed to be affected by the moving ball of fire, the flaming torches, the groupings and movements, well devised by Brook and three other directors in relation to the tomb of Ataxerxes, a two-tiered platform cut into the rock. Some of the vocal sounds were moving, many were striking. But the reactions of most spectators seem to have been tarnished by a resentful awareness of missing out on the meaning. Many would have guessed that it was Prometheus who was chained or roped to a ledge high on the rockface; not everyone understood that the shrieking girl was a vulture, or why, later on, she dragged a scared boy out of the tomb to be taught language. (This was possibly an outcropping remnant of the work done the previous year on Handke's *Kaspar*.)

John Dexter's way of working with writers is quite different, but in his production of *The Royal Hunt of the Sun*[10] on the thrust stage at Chichester, his use of sound effects, masks, and mime, his spectacular realization of the Inca rituals, his stylization of the massacre became inseparable from Peter Shaffer's scripting of the sequences. In *Equus*[11] Dexter's decision to seat a jury of spectators on stage above the action was partly to try to approximate Chichester conditions, with audience surrounding the action.

The greatest flexibility in working conditions is to be found in the fringe, and it is here that most attempts have been made to establish collaborative relationships between author, director, and actors. In 1970, having found that the

[10] See above, pp. 52–3.
[11] See above, pp. 54–5.

three-weekly changeover system allowed too little time for preparatory work on the text, Max Stafford-Clark resigned as artistic director of the Traverse Theatre, Edinburgh, to form a subsidiary company, the Traverse Theatre Workshop, in which he always had a long period of preparation with playwright, actors, and musicians before presenting a play in public, afterwards withdrawing it for more work to be done on it before showing it again. Howard Brenton's *Hitler Dances* (produced 1972) was evolved in this way. When rehearsals began in October 1971 none of the text was written. It was built partly from the actors' improvisations and autobiographical reminiscences, partly by Brenton's writing. After it was staged it was withdrawn and collaboratively reworked several times before the script reached its final version. Max Stafford-Clark also involved the playwrights John Spurling and Stanley Eveling in collaborative work before the group was disbanded.

This method of working had already been used successfully during the Sixties by the American director Joseph Chaikin, who involved Jean-Claude van Itallie, Susan Yankowitz, and other writers in close collaborative work with the actors and musicians of the Open Theatre. The great advantage is that, becoming familiar with the personalities, voices, styles, and techniques of the actors, the writer finds himself in possession of a repertoire of images and sounds, which adds up to a physical vocabulary. Stafford-Clark went on to found the Joint Stock Company in 1974 with William Gaskill and David Aukin. Working with Brenton, Heathcote Williams, David Hare, Caryl Churchill, and Barrie Keeffe, Stafford-Clark and Gaskill have involved the writers in collaborative preparatory work with the actors. But not nearly enough attempts are being made to break down the convention by which a script is completed before it is shown to the director and actors.

Some interesting work has been done on the fringe by directors who have dispensed with playwrights, building up a script out of improvisation. If every production is a chain of impacts, every rehearsal should be an opportunity to dismantle part of it. An advantage of working without a writer is that director and actors are left free to scrap some links and reforge others. As in *camera stylo* films, the director needs to be something of an author himself. Mike Leigh had experience as a drama student, as an art student, and as an unsuccessful playwright before he began directing improvisationally. He found as an art student that what he had not experienced as an actor was 'the whole thing of the creative experience being something that's unpredictable but controlled—you're actually discovering something new.'[12] He starts by giving his actors an outline of a character, inviting them to fill it in from their own experience or from people they have known. Plot evolves out of what happens in rehearsal. 'The whole thing hinges on not letting anything become holy or definitive until it's crossed over into the area of potentially dramatic or theatrical imagery. Even then you can change it.'

Mike Bradwell, who has been working in a similar way with the Hull Truck Company since 1971, was an actor in Mike Leigh's *Bleak Moments*. In Mike Bradwell's work, unlike Mike Leigh's, the action is regularly interrupted by songs, which alters the problem of shaping the narrative material. It also, unfortunately, tends to limit the possibilities of exploring the situations in depth, because it breaks the narrative into segments. Where behaviour, for the writer, is only the outward expression of an inner process, for the actor it is the coinage he is used to dealing in. The danger of improvisation is that the actor thinks more in terms of impact on the audience than of what might lie behind everything the character says and does.

Steven Berkoff does not construct mainly through improvisation, but the success of *East* (produced 1975) depended partly on his having worked for about three years with his London Theatre Group, building up a physical language, visual effects the actors could produce by mime, posture, and grouping, sound effects they could produce without mechanical aids. In Berkoff's adaptation of Poe's *The Fall of the House of Usher*, he physicalized the decrepit

---

[12] Interview with Ronald Hayman, *The Times*, 7 Aug. 1974.

house, creaking eerily as the floorboards. In *East* he played a noisy motor cycle. In his adaptations of Kafka, Aeschylus, and Strindberg, he tended to apply the same mime techniques to each classic; matter was eclipsed by manner. But in *East* he devised the matter for the manner, writing a script partly in pseudo-Shakespearian blank verse and developing much of the action, obviously, out of improvisation.

The Shakespeare parody depended a little too heavily on lurching from pretentious archaism into modern colloquial obscenity. 'Piss off, thou lump' was one characteristic phrase. But even writing on this level can be redeemed by good acting, and there were some hilarious mimes that inflated first the male and then the female sex organs to surreal dimensions. The first mime involved a movement of hauling it in like invisible rope before the actor zipped up his flies; the second a movement of groping about as if inside a dark cave. There was another good piece of obscene mime after the mother (played by an actor in drag) had given an amusing account of being groped by her own son in a dark cinema. But generally our fringe groups have profited little from discoveries made by such American groups as Joseph Chaikin's Open Theatre.

In mainstream theatre, too, there has been little transatlantic interaction. Edward Albee has borrowed from T. S. Eliot and Harold Pinter, but British playwrights have taken little notice of the American example. On the fringe, though, we have had one-way traffic in the opposite direction. Off-Broadway is much older than its English counterpart, which is largely the creation of refugees from the States—Charles Marowitz, Jim Haynes, Ed Berman, Nancy Meckler. Of the many attempts to launch Off-Broadway-type theatres in London during the Fifties, the most determined was made by Charles Marowitz, who in 1957 started a group he called In-Stage, producing plays in a tiny angular theatre inside the British Drama League building in Fitzroy Square. He went on working with different actors in different spaces until in 1968 he got possession of a cellar in

Tottenham Court Road, which he called the Open Space.

In 1963 Jim Haynes opened the Traverse Theatre Club, which had 60 seats, in an Edinburgh tenement, where he built up a large young audience for small-scale productions of offbeat plays, including many by new or *avant-garde* writers. The Traverse served as the model for the small theatres which spread like a cellular structure over England and Scotland during the next few years. The Close Theatre, a studio offshoot of the Glasgow Citizens' Theatre, was the first, and this, in turn, served as the model for the studio theatres developed by the larger English repertory theatres.

In 1968 Ed Berman, an ex-Rhodes scholar, set up Inter-Action as a trust 'with the central aim of making the arts, especially drama, more relevant to urban community life and working to break down the cultural barriers that exist in group situations.' He had already been writing and directing plays for the Mercury Theatre in Notting Hill; by the end of 1968 he had started a street theatre group, Doggs Troupe, and launched a season of lunch-hour productions in the basement of a Queensway restaurant. His success helped to encourage the proliferation of lunch-hour theatres. Like Jim Haynes, Berman has influenced the way our fringe has developed by inviting foreign companies which have served as models.

It was Haynes who arranged for the 1967 visit of the company from the most influential Off-Broadway theatre, Ellen Stewart's Café La Mama. Soon there was a London La Mama running workshops in what it called La Mama techniques. The Wherehouse/La Mama company was started by two Americans who had acted at the Café La Mama, and within its first year eight actors had splintered off to form themselves into a group under Nancy Meckler's direction called the Freehold. Using techniques very similar to those of such New York directors as Joseph Chaikin, Tom O'Horgan, and Richard Schechner, the group began to explore the actors' physical and vocal powers of expression. A sentence of dialogue might be atomized into isolated sounds. Distending the vowels, playing with the consonants, the actors would use their voices and their bodies to find coefficients for what was lost as the words became unintelligible. The company achieved its greatest success with its 1969–70 reworking of Sophocles' *Antigone*, doing particularly well with the choruses. Usually it is hard for contemporary actors to speak chorically with any conviction, but in this production the sense of the words was subordinated to the sounds, while the main statement was made through movement. The inspired gymnastic choreography took its rhythm from the words, but the audience was most aware of the shifting patterns formed by the actors' bodies. Individuality was sunk into a *mêlée* of limbs.

If I had been writing a book like this one in the early Fifties, it would not have been necessary to devote much space to directors or groups. The necessity is an index of the way theatre has followed Artaud's prescription, giving the director a more authorial function, closer to the function he has in the cinema. Though, in London, most plays are still being staged in old-fashioned proscenium theatres, less depends on scenery, more on theatrical images evolved in rehearsal, using the actors' bodies in sequences conceived by authors and modelled by directors. Very few phrases from contemporary plays lodge themselves in the memory as Shakespearian phrases do. What we mostly remember are theatrical moments such as the flagellation of the Marquis de Sade with Charlotte Corday's hair or an old man cackling at the ruminations of his younger self on a tape-recorder or a black girl using a trephine to bore a hole into a man's skull. The first of these three moments was based on a suggestion by the actress, Glenda Jackson. Peter Brook's main contribution was the introduction of quasi-orchestral whistling by the surrounding lunatics to convey the sound of a whiplash cutting through the air. The other two images were created by writers, but the words involved were of secondary importance.

As the power of the word has dwindled, the theatre has gained greatly in flexibility. Many of the new theatre buildings allow for the shape of the acting area to be modified according to the requirements of the production; nearly all the new buildings encourage a more fluid relationship between performer and public. At the same time, ideas of form have become less rigid. The barriers between the arts have largely been broken down, stylistic impurity has been cultivated, and it is already quite hard to remember how recently playwrights were voluntarily observing the unities of time, place, and action.

As songs, jokes, and vaudeville techniques have bulked larger, less has come to depend on narrative. Even the actor's identity no longer disappears so completely into the role. Generally, theatre is more like a forum in which the performer invites the public to participate in a game of 'How would you behave if you were in a situation like this one?' In the Shakespearian theatre the audience was also being invited to participate in a game, but the rules were different. At the beginning of *Henry V* the Chorus promises that the actors will 'On your imaginary forces work' and he invites the spectators to

> Piece out our imperfections with your thoughts. . . .
> For 'tis your thoughts that now must deck our kings,
> Carry them here and there: jumping o'er times;
> Turning th'accomplishment of many years
> Into an hour-glass

The main trouble with the games played in the contemporary theatre is that too little is left to the imagination. There is too little mutual stimulus between actor and spectator, and too little mutual trust.

Television is conducive to mental laziness because it does nothing to work on the viewer's imaginary forces, but I believe audiences are not only capable of more imaginative effort than they are usually required to make, but eager for the challenge and the opportunity. What makes our unadventurousness all the more pathetic is that experiment could be more fruitful than ever before. The best hope for the future is that there will be much more collaborative creation between writers, directors, and actors, and that audiences will be drawn more creatively into the collaboration.

Appendix: Year by year 1955-78

1955

What turned out to be the most important theatrical event of the year was the production of Beckett's *Waiting for Godot* at the Arts Theatre in August, more than two and a half years after its Paris premiere (January 1953). It was directed at the Arts by Peter Hall, who had been given artistic control of the theatre in January, after a year as assistant director.

In the West End Terence Rattigan's 1954 double bill *Separate Tables* was still running. At the Lyric, Hammersmith, Peter Brook directed *The Lark*, Christopher Fry's adaptation of Anouilh's *L'Alouette*, in May, and it was running at the same time as Giraudoux's *Tiger at the Gates*, also in Fry's adaptation. J. B. Priestley's *Mr. Kettle and Mrs. Moon* opened in September, directed by Tony Richardson. At Stratford-on-Avon Brook directed *Titus Andronicus* with Olivier and Vivien Leigh. Joan Littlewood had moved her company, Theatre Workshop, into the Theatre Royal, Stratford East, at the end of 1953, and her 1955 productions there included *Richard II, Volpone*, and Labiche's *The Italian Straw Hat*. In June, at the Devon Festival, Barnstaple, she directed Brecht's *Mother Courage* playing the name part herself.

1956

In April the English Stage Company opened at the Royal Court Theatre with George Devine as its artistic director and Tony Richardson as his associate. The first production was Angus Wilson's *The Mulberry Bush*, which was performed in repertoire with Arthur Miller's 1953 play *The Crucible*. In May John Osborne's *Look Back in Anger* was introduced into the repertoire, together with a double bill by Ronald Duncan, *Don Juan* and *The Death of Satan*. Nigel Dennis's adaptation of his novel *Cards of Identity* followed in June, and Brecht's *The Good Woman of Setzuan* in October.

In August, when the Berliner Ensemble began its season at the Palace Theatre, Brecht's *Der Kaukasische Kreidekreis* was seen in his own production, together with *Mutter Courage*, which he had co-directed with Erich Engel, and *Pauken und Trompeten*, an adaptation of Farquhar's *The Recruiting Officer*.

Brendan Behan's first play, *The Quare Fellow*, was produced at Stratford East by Joan Littlewood, and Dylan Thomas's *Under Milk Wood*, which had been broadcast in 1954, was staged by Douglas Cleverdon and Edward Burnham at the New.

At the Phoenix Theatre Peter Brook directed three plays starring Paul Scofield—*Hamlet*; an adaptation by Dennis Cannan and Pierre Bost of Graham Greene's 1940 novel *The Power and the Glory*; and a revival of T. S. Eliot's 1939 play *The Family Reunion*. Enid Bagnold's *The Chalk Garden* had a long run in the West End, as did Peter Ustinov's *Romanoff and Juliet* and Noël Coward's *Nude with Violin*. Joan Littlewood's other productions at Stratford East included Marlowe's *Edward II* and an adaptation of Hasek's *The Good Soldier Schweik*.

1957

Osborne's *The Entertainer* was staged at the Royal Court in April, directed by Tony Richardson, but the company's search for new English playwrights was unproductive. Nigel Dennis's *The Making of Moo* was given a full-scale production in June, directed by Tony Richardson, but the most important innovation of the year was the Sunday night productions without décor. At a cost of about £100 each, five plays were tried out, including John Arden's *The Waters of Babylon*, and N. F. Simpson's *A Resounding Tinkle*.

Robert Bolt's first play to be produced, *The Critic and the Heart*, was seen at Oxford in April, and in November his second, *Flowering Cherry*, opened in the West End. At Stratford East Joan Littlewood staged Henry Chapman's *You Won't Always Be on Top* in October.

1958

Harold Pinter's *The Birthday Party* was presented at the Lyric, Hammersmith, directed by Peter Wood, but survived for only 16 performances. Arnold Wesker's *Chicken Soup with Barley* was seen at the Royal Court in July, but only for a week, and only as part of a four-week season in which provincial repertory companies were bringing productions to London. (John Dexter had directed *Chicken Soup with Barley* at the Belgrade Theatre, Coventry.) The English Stage Company's own productions at the Court included *Epitaph for George Dillon* by John Osborne and Anthony Creighton, and Ann Jellicoe's *The Sport of My Mad Mother* which she co-directed with George Devine later in the month. In April N. F. Simpson's *A Resounding Tinkle* was presented in a double bill with his *The Hole*, both directed by William Gaskill. John Arden's *Live Like Pigs* was co-directed by George Devine and Anthony Page in September. There were Sunday night productions of Doris Lessing's *Each His Own Wilderness* and Donald Howarth's *Lady on the Barometer*.

In the West End too, there was a sudden proliferation of new English plays: N. C. Hunter's *A Touch of the Sun*, Graham Greene's *The Potting Shed*, Terence Rattigan's *Variation on a Theme*, Jane Arden's *The Party*, and Peter Shaffer's *Five Finger Exercise*. John Mortimer's double bill *The Dock Brief* and *What Shall We Tell Caroline?* transferred to the West End from the Lyric, Hammersmith, and Bernard Kops's *The Hamlet of Stepney Green* transferred from Oxford to the Lyric, Hammersmith. T. S. Eliot's last play *The Elder Statesman* opened at the Edinburgh Festival, transferring to the West End.

At Stratford East Joan Littlewood's productions included Shelagh Delaney's *A Taste of Honey* and Brendan Behan's *The Hostage*; both transferred to the West End.

1959

John Dexter directed Wesker's *Roots* in Coventry with Joan Plowright, and the production played at the Royal Court for four weeks, transferring to the West End. Donald Howarth's *Lady on the Barometer* was given a full-scale production under the new title *Sugar in the Morning*. Willis Hall's *The Long and the Short and the Tall* was directed by Lindsay Anderson, and it transferred to the New. In October John Arden's *Serjeant Musgrave's Dance* was directed by Lindsay Anderson. Sunday night productions included Wesker's *The Kitchen* directed by Dexter.

Productions at the Lyric, Hammersmith, included Alun Owen's *The Rough and Ready Lot*, and Willis Hall's double bill *Last Day in Dreamland* and *A Glimpse of the Sea*, directed by John Dexter.

In the West End there were relatively few new English plays, but Graham Greene's *The Complaisant Lover* was directed by John Gielgud, and John Osborne directed his own musical *The World of Paul Slickey* which opened in May, after a provincial tour, but survived for only 47 performances.

The Mermaid, London's first large postwar theatre, was opened in May.

1960

The Governors of the Shakespeare Memorial Theatre, Stratford-on-Avon, appointed Peter Hall as artistic director, and the company opened its first London season at the Aldwych in December with Donald McWhinnie's production of *The Duchess of Malfi*.

A Pinter double bill consisting of *The Room* and *The Dumb Waiter* was presented at the Hampstead Theatre Club, transferring to the Royal Court. There, in June and July, the Wesker trilogy (*Chicken Soup with Barley, Roots* and *I'm Talking about Jerusalem*) was staged by John Dexter. In September *The Happy Haven* by John Arden and Margaretta D'Arcy was directed by William Gaskill.

Sunday night productions included a Christopher Logue double bill, *Trials by Logue,* and Gwyn Thomas's *The Keep*.

In the West End Pinter's *The Caretaker*, directed by Donald McWhinnie, opened in May to run for nearly a year. Robert Bolt's *A Man for All Seasons* opened in July, and it had 320 performances. In August another of Bolt's plays, *The Tiger and the Horse*, opened at the Queen's. Peter Hall directed John Mortimer's *The Wrong Side of the Park*, and Terence Rattigan's *Ross* started its long run at the Haymarket in May. *Billy Liar* by Keith Waterhouse and Willis Hall was directed by Lindsay Anderson, and Noël Coward's *Waiting in the Wings* opened.

At Stratford East Joan Littlewood directed Stephen Lewis's *Sparrers Can't Sing* in August, and in November William Kotcheff directed Alun Owen's *Progress to the Park*.

1961

The company under Peter Hall's control at Stratford and the Aldwych acquired the title Royal Shakespeare Company, and the first new play it produced in London was John Whiting's *The Devils*, which Peter Wood directed at the Aldwych in February.

At the Royal Court Wesker's *The Kitchen* was given a full-scale production in June, again directed by Dexter, and John Osborne's *Luther* was directed by Tony Richardson in July. In September it transferred to the Phoenix, and, at the Court, George Devine directed Nigel Dennis's *August for the People*.

Progress to the Park opened in the West End. Apart from *Luther* and the Stratford East transfers, there were few serious new British plays running there. The revue *Beyond the Fringe*, which had been at the 1960 Edinburgh Festival, opened at the Fortune in June.

1962

The Chichester Festival Theatre, the first large theatre to be built in Britain with a thrust stage, opened in July with Laurence Olivier as artistic director.

The RSC ran an experimental season at the Arts Theatre. In March Donald McWhinnie directed Giles Cooper's *Everything in the Garden*. Subsequent productions included

Henry Livings's *Nil Carborundum*, David Rudkin's *Afore Night Come*, and *Infanticide in the House of Fred Ginger* by Fred Watson.

At the Royal Court Ann Jellicoe co-directed her play *The Knack* with Keith Johnstone, and John Dexter directed Wesker's *Chips with Everything*, which transferred to the West End. John Osborne's *Plays for England* were produced: *The Blood of the Bambergs* was directed by John Dexter and *Under Plain Cover* by Jonathan Miller. Sunday night productions included *The Pope's Wedding* by Edward Bond.

At the Aldwych Pinter co-directed his *The Collection* with Peter Hall in June. John Whiting's 1951 play *A Penny for a Song* was revived in a new version, and Christopher Fry's *Curtmantle* was produced.

In the West End, Doris Lessing's *Play with a Tiger* and John Mortimer's *Two Stars for Comfort* were produced. Peter Ustinov co-directed his own play *Photo Finish* with Nicholas Garland at the Saville. In May Peter Shaffer's double bill *The Private Ear and the Public Eye* was directed by Peter Wood.

David Turner's *The Bedmakers* was produced at Coventry, as was his *Semi-Detached*, which had a West End run later in the year with Olivier in the cast.

1963

The National Theatre opened at the Old Vic in October with *Hamlet* directed by Olivier.

At the Royal Court Gwyn Thomas's *Jackie the Jumper* and Henry Livings's *Kelly's Eye* were produced, and Ann Jellicoe, who directed Barry Reckord's *Skyvers* as a Sunday night production, gave it a full-scale production later in the year.

Pinter directed a double bill of his own plays *The Lover* and *The Dwarfs* at the Arts. James Saunders's *Next Time I'll Sing to You* opened there and transferred to the West End. Charles Wood's *Cockade*, consisting of three one-act plays, *Prisoner and Escort*, *John Thomas*, and *Spare*, was also produced at the Arts.

Three Mermaid productions transferred to the West End, two of them plays by Bill Naughton—*All in Good Time* and *Alfie*. The third was *The Bed Sitting Room*, written and directed by John Antrobus and Spike Milligan.

Joan Littlewood's production of *Oh What a Lovely War* opened at Stratford East in March, transferring to Wyndham's in June.

The Bristol Old Vic's production of *A Severed Head* by Iris Murdoch and J. B. Priestley transferred to the West End, where the other main productions of the year were Terence Rattigan's *Man and Boy*, Giles Cooper's *Out of the Crocodile*, and Robert Bolt's *Gentle Jack*.

In Edinburgh Jim Haynes opened the Traverse Theatre Club during January and the first British 'Happening' was staged at the Festival in the autumn by Ken Dewey, Alan Kaprow and Charles Marowitz.

In Stoke-on-Trent Alan Ayckbourn directed his play *Mr. Whatnot* in November.

1964

In July at the Chichester Festival the National Theatre presented its first new play, Peter Shaffer's *The Royal Hunt of the Sun*, directed by John Dexter and Desmond O'Donovan. It transferred to the Old Vic in December.

At the Royal Court John Osborne's *Inadmissible Evidence* was directed by Anthony Page.

At the Aldwych in July the RSC presented *Expeditions One*, consisting of James Saunders's *The Pedagogue*, Jean Tardieu's *The Keyhole*, Beckett's *Act Without Words II*, Arrabal's *Picnic on the Battlefield*, and John Whiting's *No Why*. In October Peter Hall directed Henry Livings's *Eh?*

Joe Orton's *Entertaining Mr. Sloane* and Frank Marcus's *The Formation Dancers*, which both opened at the Arts, both transferred to the West End. Graham Greene's *Carving a Statue* and James Saunders's *A Scent of Flowers* opened in the autumn.

John Arden's *Armstrong's Last Goodnight* was premiered at the Glasgow Citizens' Theatre.

The RSC's *Theatre of Cruelty* season was at the LAMDA Theatre, directed by Peter Brook and Charles Marowitz.

1965

The National Theatre presented *Armstrong's Last Goodnight* at Chichester in July, directed by John Dexter and William Gaskill, and later in the month Peter Shaffer's *Black Comedy* was directed by Dexter.

At the Aldwych *Expeditions Two* opened in February, including Charles Wood's *Don't Make Me Laugh*, Johnny Speight's *If There Weren't Any Blacks You'd Have to Invent Them*, and David Mercer's *The Governor's Lady*. Pinter's *The Homecoming* was directed by Peter Hall in June.

At the Royal Court John Osborne directed Charles Wood's *Meals on Wheels* and Anthony Page directed Osborne's *A Patriot for Me*. After William Gaskill had taken over as Artistic Director he staged Edward Bond's *Saved*, in a repertory that also included N. F. Simpson's *The Cresta Run*, and Ann Jellicoe's production of her play *Shelley*.

John Arden's *Left-Handed Liberty* and Bill Naughton's *Spring and Port Wine* were produced at the Mermaid, and Donald Howarth's production of his *A Lily in Little India* opened at the Hampstead Theatre Club.

At the Arts in September the Traverse Theatre company was seen in Paul Ableman's *Green Julia*.

Inadmissible Evidence transferred belatedly to Wyndham's in March. Frank Marcus's *The Killing of Sister George* was directed by Val May at the Bristol Old Vic, transferring to the West End, where David Mercer's *Ride a Cock Horse* opened, starring Peter O'Toole. Arnold Wesker's *The Four Seasons* had a brief run.

At Stratford East Alun Owen's *A Little Winter Love* was produced.

One of the earliest fringe groups, The People Show, was formed.

1966

At the Aldwych the RSC's repertoire included Peter Brook's *US*, Charles Dyer's *Staircase*, and David Mercer's *Belcher's Luck*. At the Old Vic John Dexter directed John Osborne's

A Bond Honoured, an adaptation of Lope de Vega's *La Fianza Satisfecha*. The repertory season at the Royal Court included Arnold Wesker's *Their Very Own and Golden City*. David Halliwell's *Little Malcolm and his Struggle against the Eunuchs* ran for a week in September. Sunday night productions included Heathcote Williams's *The Local Stigmatic*, directed by Peter Gill in March, Christopher Hampton's *When Did You Last See My Mother?* in June, and in August, Joe Orton's *It's My Criminal* and *The Ruffian on the Stair*.

At the Hampstead Theatre Club, productions included John McGrath's *Events while Guarding the Bofors Gun*, Giles Cooper's *Happy Family*, John Bowen's *After the Rain*, Michael Hastings's *The Silence of Lee Harvey Oswald*, and Colin Spencer's *The Ballad of the False Barman*. In the London Traverse Company's season at the Jeanetta Cochrane Theatre, Charles Marowitz directed Joe Orton's *Loot*.

In the West End Noël Coward's *Suite in Three Keys*, a group of three plays, was produced.

QUIPU, the first lunch-time theatre group, was started by David Halliwell.

1967

The National Theatre produced Tom Stoppard's *Rosencrantz and Guildenstern Are Dead* at the Old Vic. A Joe Orton double bill, combining *The Ruffian on the Stair* with *The Erpingham Camp*, was seen at the Royal Court, as were David Storey's *The Restoration of Arnold Middleton*, Donald Howarth's *Ogodiveleftthegason*, and Charles Wood's *Dingo*.

Frank Marcus's *Studies of the Nude* was produced at the Hampstead Theatre Club, as were James Kennaway's *Country Dance* and Jack Pulman's *The Happy Apple*. C. P. Taylor's *Who's Pinkus? Where's Chelm?* and Peter Terson's *The Mighty Reservoy* were produced at the Jeanetta Cochrane Theatre.

West End productions included John Mortimer's *The Judge*, Alan Ayckbourn's *Relatively Speaking*, *A Day in the Death of Joe Egg* by Peter Nichols, Robert Shaw's *The Man in the Glass Booth*, Brian Friel's *Philadelphia Here I Come*, Charles Wood's *Fill the Stage with Happy Hours*, and Simon Gray's *Wise Child*.

1968

There were no premieres of British plays by the RSC or the National Theatre, except for John Lennon's *In His Own Write* as part of a triple bill at the Old Vic. At the Royal Court John Osborne's *Time Present* was followed by his *Hotel in Amsterdam*. Other productions included Christopher Hampton's *Total Eclipse*, and John Hopkins's *This Story of Yours*.

Hampstead Theatre Club produced John McGrath's *Bakke's Night of Fame* (an adaptation of William Butler's novel *A Danish Gambit*), John Bowen's *Little Boxes*, and Peter Terson's *Mooney and His Caravans*, Richard Eyre's dramatization of Jennifer Dawson's novel *The Ha-ha*, Colin Spencer's *Spitting Image*, John Hale's *It's All in the Mind*, and Stanley Eveling's *The Strange Case of Martin Richter*.

The Hero Rises Up by John Arden and Margaretta D'Arcy was directed by the authors at the Round House, and Arden's *Harold Muggins Is a Martyr* was produced at the Unity Theatre.

At the Chichester Festival Peter Ustinov directed his own play *The Unknown Soldier and His Wife* in May.

At the Mermaid Peter Luke's *Hadrian VII*, adapted from the novel by Fr. Rolfe, Baron Corvo, was directed by Peter Dews.

Two Bristol Old Vic productions transferred to the West End: *The Italian Girl*, adapted by James Saunders and Iris Murdoch from her novel, and Frank Marcus's *Mrs. Mouse Are You Within?* Other West End productions included Peter Shaffer's *The White Liars* (in a double bill with his *Black Comedy*), Tom Stoppard's *Enter a Free Man*, his *The Real Inspector Hound*, and Alan Bennett's *40 Years On*.

The Open Space Theatre in Tottenham Court Road opened under Charles Marowitz's direction in July with his production of John Herbert's *Fortune and Men's Eyes*, which transferred to the Comedy.

Michael Croft directed Peter Terson's *The Apprentices* at the Jeanetta Cochrane Theatre in August.

Henvy Livings directed his own play *The Little Mrs. Foster Show* at the Nottingham Playhouse, and Edward Bond's *Narrow Road to the Deep North* was produced in Coventry.

Jim Haynes opened his Arts Lab in Drury Lane, and by the end of the year many new fringe groups had been formed, including Portable Theatre, Inter-Action, the Pip Simmons Group, the Wherehouse Company, the Brighton Combination, and Incubus. The Royal Court opened its Theatre Upstairs, and Inter-Action (together with Theatre-scope) opened the Ambiance Lunch Hour Theatre Club.

1969

The National Theatre produced Charles Wood's *H: Monologues at Front of Burning Cities* at the Old Vic, and presented an experimental season at the Jeanetta Cochrane Theatre, where John Spurling's *Macrune's Guevara* and Maureen Duffy's *Rites* were produced. In October Peter Nichols's *The National Health* was staged at the Old Vic. For the RSC Peter Hall directed Simon Gray's *Dutch Uncle* in March and Pinter's double bill *Landscape* and *Silence* in July.

In the Edward Bond season which opened in February at the Royal Court Jane Howell directed *Narrow Road to the Deep North* and William Gaskill directed *Early Morning* and *Saved*. Lindsay Anderson directed two plays by David Storey—*In Celebration* and *The Contractor*.

Productions at the Theatre Upstairs included Mike Stott's *Erogenous Zones*, Barry Hanson's *The Enoch Show*, Peter Gill's *Over Gardens Out* and *Sleepers' Den*, and Stanley Eveling's *Dear Janet Rosenburg Dear Mr. Kooning*.

Peter Barnes's *The Ruling Class*, which had been produced at the Nottingham Playhouse, opened in the West End, where Joe Orton's *What the Butler Saw* and Ann Jellicoe's *The Giveaway* were produced. In May Henry

Livings's *Honour and Offer* was directed by John Neville at the Fortune, the first play in a new season. The second was Roy Minton's *Sometimes Never*. Alun Owen's *There'll Be Some Changes Made* was directed by Donald McWhinnie in September, and Ted Allan's *I've Seen You Cut Lemons* opened in December.

Frank Marcus's *The Window* and David Halliwell's *A Who's Who of Flapland* were produced at the Ambiance. Halliwell's *K. D. Dufford Hears K. D. Dufford Ask K. D. Dufford how K. D. Dufford'll Make K. D. Dufford* was produced at the LAMDA Theatre. The Freehold presented a double bill, *Mr. Jello* and *Alternatives*, at the Mercury. At the Open Space Peter Barnes's double bill *Leonardo's Last Supper* and *Noonday Demons* was directed by Charles Marowitz. Michael Croft's National Youth Theatre production of Peter Terson's *Fuzz* opened at the Jeanetta Cochrane Theatre.

The theatre at Greenwich opened in October with a production by the artistic director, Ewan Hooper, of his own documentary *Martin Luther King*.

Many new fringe groups were formed, including Max Stafford-Clark's Traverse Theatre Workshop, the Freehold, Naftali Yavin's TOC (The Other Company), Steven Berkoff's London Theatre Group, and Keith Johnstone's Theatre Machine.

1970

The RSC presented David Mercer's *After Haggerty* at the Aldwych. Royal Court productions included Donald Howarth's *Three Months Gone*, David Storey's *The Contractor* and his *Home*, Christopher Hampton's *The Philanthropist*, and Heathcote Williams's *AC/DC*.

At the Theatre Upstairs Howard Brenton's *Cheek* was directed by William Gaskill in June, and later in the month Portable Theatre presented a double bill consisting of Brenton's *Fruit* and David Hare's *What Happened to Blake?* In November Howard Barker's *No-One Was Saved* was produced.

David Hare's *Slag* was staged at the Hampstead Theatre

Club. Peter Hall directed Peter Shaffer's *The Battle of Shrivings* in the West End, where other productions included David Mercer's *Flint*, four plays by Michael Frayn under the title *The Two of Us*, Alan Ayckbourn's *How the Other Half Loves*, and Pinter's television plays *Tea Party* and *The Basement*.

Robert Bolt's *Vivat! Vivat Regina!* was produced at the Chichester Festival, afterwards transferring to the West End.

Arnold Wesker directed his play *The Friends* at the Round House, where *Oh! Calcutta!*, devised by Kenneth Tynan, was staged before transferring to the West End.

Christopher Fry's *A Yard of Sun* was produced at the Nottingham Playhouse and seen at the Old Vic for a week.

At the Open Space John Hopkins's *Find Your Way Home* was produced. At the Green Banana Restaurant Inter-Action presented Howard Brenton's *Heads* and *The Education of Skinny Spew* and Tom Stoppard's *After Magritte*.

Peter Terson's *The Whitby Lifeboat Disaster* was directed by Peter Cheeseman at Stoke-on-Trent in May. The production was seen at the Royal Court later in the year as part of the 'Come Together' Festival of fringe events. At Greenwich John Mortimer's *A Voyage Around My Father* was directed by Claude Watham.

Several new fringe companies were formed, including Ken Campbell's Road Show, Belt and Braces, and Low Moan Spectacular. The Young Vic Theatre was opened, as was the Soho Theatre, which later became the Soho Poly.

1971

The RSC presented David Mercer's *After Haggerty*, and Pinter's *Old Times* directed by Peter Hall. In October, during a season at The Place, Trevor Griffiths's *Occupations* was directed by Buzz Goodbody.

At the Royal Court John Osborne's *West of Suez* was directed by Anthony Page, and David Storey's *The Changing Room* by Lindsay Anderson. At the Theatre Upstairs Snoo Wilson directed *Lay-By* by David Hare, Trevor Griffiths, and five other writers.

Two of Simon Gray's plays were produced in the West End: *Spoiled* and *Butley*, the latter directed by Harold Pinter. Other productions included E. A. Whitehead's *The Foursome*.

At Greenwich productions included Peter Nichols's *Forget-Me-Not Lane* and Michael Frayn's *The Sandboy*.

New groups included The General Will with David Edgar as one of the organizers, and the Portable Theatre Workshop, directed by Malcolm Griffiths. The theatre in the Islington pub The King's Head was opened, as was Basement Theatre. A Fringe Festival was organized in the Cockpit Theatre by David Aukin, but it did not become an annual event.

Fringe productions included John McGrath's *Plugged in to History* and *Trees in the Wind*, David Edgar's *The National Interest* and *Tedderella*, and John Grillo's *Blubber*.

1972

In February Tom Stoppard's *Jumpers* was directed by Peter Wood at the Old Vic for the National Theatre, and in December the RSC produced *The Island of the Mighty* by John Arden and Margaretta D'Arcy at the Aldwych.

Productions at the Royal Court included E. A. Whitehead's *Alpha Beta*, Charles Wood's *Veterans*, Arnold Wesker's *The Old Ones*, Edna O'Brien's *A Pagan Place*, and John Osborne's *A Sense of Detachment*.

At the Theatre Upstairs productions included *A Fart for Europe* by Howard Brenton and David Edgar, N. F. Simpson's *Was He Anyone?*, and Caryl Churchill's *Owners*.

At Hampstead Theatre Club David Hare's *The Great Exhibition* was produced.

West End productions included Frank Marcus's *Notes on a Love Affair*, John Mortimer's *I Claudius*, and Alan Ayckbourn's *Time and Time Again*.

At Stratford East Henry Livings directed his own play *Finest Family in the Land*. Trevor Griffiths's *Sam Sam* and Howard Barker's *Alpha Alpha* were produced at the Open Space. John McGrath's *A Fish in the Sea* was produced at Liverpool.

New groups formed included the Hull Truck Company, the 7:84 Theatre Company, the Common Stock Theatre Company, the Wakefield Tricycle Company, and Foco Novo.

The Half Moon Theatre opened in the East End, and the Almost Free Theatre in Rupert Street, London W.1.

Fringe productions included David Edgar's *State of Emergency* and his *Death Story*, Portable Theatre's collectively written *England's Ireland*, and John McGrath's *Underneath* and *Serjeant Musgrave Dances On*.

1973

The National Theatre produced Peter Shaffer's *Equus* and Trevor Griffiths's *The Party*. Both were directed by John Dexter. The RSC produced Pinter's *Landscape* and *Silence* at the Aldwych, directed by Peter Hall.

Royal Court productions included Christopher Hampton's *Savages*, Edward Bond's *The Sea*, Howard Brenton's *Magnificence*, and two plays by David Storey: *Cromwell* and *The Farm*.

West End productions included John Mortimer's *Collaborators*, Alan Bennett's *Habeas Corpus*, Alan Ayckbourn's *Absurd Person Singular*, and Terence Rattigan's double bill *In Praise of Love*.

Joan Littlewood directed Peter Rankin's *So You Want to Be in Pictures?* at Stratford East. At the Shaw Barrie Keeffe's *Only a Game* and Peter Terson's *Geordie's March* were produced.

At Nottingham David Hare directed *Brassneck*, which he had written with Howard Brenton, and John McGrath's *Soft or a Girl* was produced.

At Exeter Jane Howell and John Dove directed Edward Bond's *Bingo*.

The Theatre at the Institute of Contemporary Arts opened. John McGrath started 7:84 Scotland.

Fringe productions included the Freehold's adaptation of Beowulf, David Rudkin's *The Filth Hunt*, Pip Simmons's *The George Jackson Black and White Minstrel Show*, John Grillo's *Snaps*, Richard O'Brien's *Rocky Horror*

Show, Irving Wardle's *The Houseboy*, Christina Brown's *Up the Bamboo Tree*, and five plays by David Edgar: *Gangsters, Baby Love, The Case of the Workers' Plane, Operation Iskra*, and *Liberated Zone*.

1974

The Royal Shakespeare Company produced David Mercer's *Duck Song*, Peter Barnes's *The Bewitched*, and Tom Stoppard's *Travesties*, directed by Peter Wood. Its productions at The Place included *The Beast* by Snoo Wilson. National Theatre productions included John Hopkins's *Next of Kin*, directed by Harold Pinter, and A. E. Ellis's *Grand Manoeuvres*.

At the Royal Court Peter Ransley's *Runaway*, David Storey's *Life Class*, and Ken Campbell's *The Great Caper* were seen in the main auditorium, and E. A. Whitehead's *The Sea Anchor* was produced at the Theatre Upstairs.

West End productions included Peter Nichols's *Chez Nous*, David Hare's *Knuckle*, Charles Lawrence's *Snap*, Peter Luke's *Bloomsbury*, and *The Golden Pathway Annual* by John Harding and John Burrows.

The Hampstead Theatre Club presented Mike Stott's *Other People*, and Ronald Eyre's *Something's Burning* was seen at the Mermaid. The National Youth Theatre produced Peter Terson's *The Trip to Florence* at the Shaw, and two plays by Paul Thompson at the Cockpit—*The Children's Crusade* and *By Common Consent*.

David Rudkin's *Ashes* was produced at the Open Space, and Heathcote Williams's *The Speakers* was staged at the ICA by the Joint Stock Company.

Alan Ayckbourn's trilogy *The Norman Conquests*, which had been premiered at Scarborough in 1973, was produced at Greenwich.

1975

The National Theatre produced Pinter's *No Man's Land*, directed by Peter Hall, and Trevor Griffiths's *Comedians*, which had been staged earlier in the year at Nottingham. RSC productions at the Aldwych included Charles Wood's

Jingo, and Graham Greene's *The Return of A. J. Raffles*.

At the Royal Court David Hare directed his own *Teeth 'n' Smiles*. Other productions included Howard Barker's *Stripwell*, Edward Bond's *The Fool*, directed by Peter Gill, and, at the Theatre Upstairs, Stephen Poliakoff's *Heroes*.

Michael Frayn's *Alphabetical Order* was produced at Hampstead Theatre Club, and, at the Open Space, Howard Barker's *Claw*. Stephen Poliakoff's *Hitting Town* and *City Sugar* were produced at the Bush, and, at the ICA, the Pip Simmons Group's *An die Musik*, and Mike Leigh's *Babies Grow Old* which had been improvised at The Other Place in Stratford-on-Avon as part of the 1974 season.

David Hare's *Fanshen* was produced by the Joint Stock Company, and the tour opened at the Sheffield Crucible Studio.

In the John Osborne season at Greenwich, *The End of Me Old Cigar* was produced in January and his dramatization of *The Picture of Dorian Gray* in February.

David Edgar's *O Fair Jerusalem!* was produced at the Birmingham Repertory Theatre Studio, and Willy Russell's *Breezeblock Park* at the Liverpool Everyman.

Other fringe productions included John McGrath's *Lay-Off, Little Red Hen*, and *Yobbo Nowt*, David Edgar's *Summer Sports* and *The National Theatre*, Snoo Wilson's *Soul of the White Ant*, the Pip Simmons Group's *The Dream of a Ridiculous Man*, the Hull Truck Company's *Oh, What!*, Richard Crane's *Venus and Superkid, Clownmaker*, and *Bloody Neighbours*, Lawrence Collinson's *Thinking Straight*, produced by a new homosexual company, Gay Sweatshop, Barrie Keeffe's *Gem*, Charles Marowitz's *Artaud at Rodez*, Allan Drury's *The Man Himself*, Alan Bleasdale's *Fat Harold and the Last 26*, and Steven Berkoff's *East*.

1976

In March the National Theatre opened in its own building on the South Bank. Before it moved out of the Old Vic, John Osborne's *Watch It Come Down* was produced. The first new play in the new building was Howard Brenton's *Weapons of Happiness*, directed by David Hare.

Peter Brook's production of *Les Ik*, which had already been performed in French in Paris, was staged in English at the Round House.

David Edgar's *Destiny* was produced at The Other Place. Productions at the Royal Court included Christopher Hampton's *Treats*, Peter Gill's *Small Change*, and David Storey's *Mother's Day*. At the Theatre Upstairs Caryl Churchill's *Light Shining in Buckinghamshire* was produced.

Hampstead Theatre Club produced Mike Stott's *Lenz*, Michael Frayn's *Clouds*, and Pam Gems's *Dusa Fish Stas and Vi*, which had been seen at the Edinburgh Festival. Mike Stott's *Funny Peculiar* was produced at the Mermaid, and Edward Bond's *The Swing* and *Grandma Faust* at the Almost Free.

In the West End Alan Ayckbourn's *Confusions* was produced, and at Greenwich Barrie Keeffe's *Scribes*.

Other fringe productions included Tom Stoppard's *Dirty Linen* and *New-Found-Land*, Snoo Wilson's *Everest Hotel*, *The Non-Stop Connolly Cycle* by John Arden and Margaretta D'Arcy, Allan Drury's *Sparrowfall*, the Joint Stock Company's *Yesterday's News*, the Hull Truck Company's *Bridget's House*, John McGrath's *The Rat Trap*, Stewart Parker's *Spokesong*, David Edgar's *Blood Sports*, Edward Bond's *Stone*, and Barrie Keeffe's *Gotcha* and *Abide with Me*.

1977

The RSC produced Peter Nichols's *Privates on Parade* at the Aldwych and Pam Gems's *Queen Christina* at The Other Place. Its first season at the Warehouse, Covent Garden, comprised C. P. Taylor's *Bandits*, Howard Barker's *That Good Between Us*, Edward Bond's *The Bundle*, James Robson's *Factory Birds*, and Barrie Keeffe's *Frozen Assets*.

The National Theatre presented Alan Ayckbourn's *Bedroom Farce*, Robert Bolt's *State of Revolution*, Bill Bryden's *Old Movies*, Shane Connaughten's *Sir Is Winning*,

John Mackendrick's *Lavender Blue*, and Julian Mitchell's *Half Life*.

At the Royal Court the first production of the new artistic director, Stuart Burge, was Howard Barker's *Fair Slaughter*. Mary O'Malley's *Once a Catholic* and John McGrath's *Trembling Giant* were produced, and, at the Theatre Upstairs, Michael Hastings's *For the West*.

West End productions included Terence Rattigan's *Cause Celèbre*, Alan Bennett's *The Old Country*, and John Mortimer's *The Bells of Hell*. Tom Stoppard's *Every Good Boy Deserves Favour* was produced in the Royal Festival Hall.

Barrie Keeffe's *It's a Mad World, My Masters* was staged by the Joint Stock Company at the Young Vic and the Round House, where it also staged Howard Brenton's *Epsom Downs*.

Bernard Pomerance's *The Elephant Man* was seen at Hampstead Theatre Club, and Snoo Wilson's *England England* at the Jeanetta Cochrane.

Stephen Lowe's *Touched* was produced at Nottingham, Ron Hutchinson's *Says I Says He* at Sheffield, Bill Morrison's *Flying Blind* at Liverpool, Barrie Keeffe's *Barbarians* at Greenwich, Arnold Wesker's *The Wedding Feast* at Leeds, Jonathan Raban's *The Sunset Touch* at Bristol, *The Seed* by Ray Speakman and Derek Nicholls at the Birmingham Repertory Studio Theatre, and David Pownall's *Music to Murder By* at the Gulbenkian Theatre, University of Kent.

Other fringe productions included James Saunders's *The Island* and *After Liverpool*, David Edgar's *Our Own People*, Mike Leigh's improvised *Abigail's Party*, Tina Brown's *Happy Yellow*, Paul Copley's *Pillion*, Alan Bleasdale's *No More Sitting on the Old School Bench*, Robert Holman's *German Skerries*, Barrie Keeffe's *Gimme Shelter*, Snoo Wilson's *Elijah Disappearing*, and Heathcote Williams's *Hancock's Last Half Hour*.

1978

National Theatre productions included David Hare's *Plenty*, Edward Bond's *The Woman*, and Harold Pinter's *Betrayal*. At the Cottesloe Theatre Arnold Wesker directed his own adaptation of his story *Love Letters on Blue Paper*. Two dramatizations by Keith Dewhurst were staged—*Lark Rise* from Flora Thompson's book *Lark Rise at Candleford*, and *The World Turned Upside Down* from Christopher Hill's book. Charles Wood's play *Has 'Washington' Legs?* was also produced at the Cottesloe.

The new plays staged by the RSC at the Aldwych were Steve Gooch's *The Woman-Pirates Anne Bonney and Mary Read*, and David Mercer's *Cousin Vladimir*. At The Other Place, Stratford, the company presented *Piaf* by Pam Gems, and, at the Warehouse, *Frozen Assets* by Barrie Keeffe, *The Jail Diary of Albie Sachs* by David Edgar, *A and R* by Pete Atkin, *Savage Amusement* by Peter Flannery, *Shout across the River* by Stephen Poliakoff, and *Look Out Here Comes Trouble* by Mary O'Malley.

Royal Court productions included *The Glad Hand* by Snoo Wilson, *Eclipse* by Leigh Jackson, and, at the Theatre Upstairs, *Class Enemy* by Nigel Williams.

West End productions included Simon Gray's *The Rear Column*, and Tom Stoppard's *Night and Day*. At the Mermaid Brian Clarke's play *Whose Life Is It Anyway?* was followed by a run of Stoppard's *Every Good Boy Deserves Favour*, after its single performance in 1977 at the Royal Festival Hall.

Hampstead Theatre Club presented James Saunders's *Bodies* and Michael Hastings's *Gloo Joo*, which transferred to the West End. Shane Connaughten's *Sir Is Winning* was seen at the Round House Downstairs, and at the ICA, C. P. Taylor's *Withdrawal Symptoms*, and Richard O'Brien's *Disaster*. The Hull Truck Company's *Bed of Roses* was staged at the Bush, and later at the Cottesloe; its production of *The New Garbo* was seen at the King's Head.

A new theatre, the Riverside Studios, opened in Hammersmith under the artistic direction of Peter Gill, who was responsible for the opening production of *The Cherry Orchard*. Nicholas Wright's play *Treetops* was staged there, as was Stephen Lowe's adaptation of Robert Tressell's novel *The Ragged Trousered Philanthropists* in a production by the Joint Stock Company.

Ronald Harwood's play *A Family* was produced at the Royal Exchange, Manchester, before transferring to the West End. *Vandaleur's Folly* by John Arden and Margaretta D'Arcy was produced by the 7:84 Company at the Oxford Playhouse. Howard Brenton, David Hare, Trevor Griffiths, and Ken Campbell collaborated on *Deeds*, which was produced at Nottingham. Ron Hutchinson's *Eejits* was produced in Sheffield, and the Liverpool Everyman presented Mike Stott's *Comings and Goings*, which transferred to Hampstead.

Select bibliography

GENERAL

In *Revolutions in Modern English Drama* (London, 1972) Katharine J. Worth sensibly puts playwrights from Osborne to Heathcote Williams into the perspective of pre-war drama. Andrew Kennedy's *Six Dramatists in Search of a Language* (Cambridge, 1975) is a highly intelligent critique of Shaw, Eliot, Beckett, Pinter, Osborne, and Arden, concentrating on the texture of the dialogue. John Russell Taylor's *Anger and After* (London, 1962; 2nd edn., 1969) gives a detailed account of developments in English drama since *Look Back in Anger*. His *The Second Wave* (London, 1971) has chapters on Nichols, Mercer, Bond, Wood, Stoppard, Terson, Orton, and Storey, with four other chapters divided between twenty-two other playwrights. John Russell Brown's *Theatre Language: a Study of Arden, Osborne, Pinter and Wesker* (London, 1972) focuses on the way the plays come to life in performance, and he has edited *Modern British Dramatists* (Englewood Cliffs, New Jersey, 1968), a collection of critical essays and articles. Oleg Kerensky's *The New British Drama: Fourteen Playwrights since Osborne and Pinter* (London, 1977) deals uncritically with Storey, Bond, Shaffer, Nichols, Whitehead, Hampton, Ayckbourn, Gray, Stoppard, Hare, Griffiths, Brenton, Barker, and Poliakoff, but contains a good deal of interesting interview material. Peter Ansorge's *Disrupting the Spectacle* (London, 1975) tersely chronicles the development of fringe theatre.

The most useful collections of reviews are Kenneth Tynan's *Curtains* (London, 1961) which reprints most of the reviews he wrote during the Fifties, *Tynan Right and Left* (London, 1967) which is not entirely devoted to play criticism but contains 200 pages of reviews written between 1957 and 1966, *John Whiting on Theatre* (London, 1966) which reprints the reviews he wrote for *The London Magazine* from 1961 to 1963, *Contemporary Theatre* edited by Geoffrey Morgan (London, 1968), an anthology of reviews written by various critics during 1966–7, and Charles Marowitz's *Confessions of a Counterfeit Critic* (London, 1973) which reprints reviews he wrote between 1958 and 1971, together with afterthoughts.

John Elsom's *Post-War British Theatre* (London, 1976) is a compendious account of the theatrical set-up, with several chapters on playwrights. Laurence Kitchin's *Drama in the Sixties* (London, 1966) focuses mainly on acting, but gives some space to writing.

The most useful collections of interviews are *The Playwrights Speak*, edited by Walter Wager (London, 1969), which contains interviews with Pinter, Osborne, Arden, and Wesker, among other, non-British playwrights, and Judith Cook's *Directors' Theatre* (London, 1974), which collects her interviews with John Barton, Peter Brook, Peter Cheeseman, John Dexter, Ronald Eyre, Patrick Garland, Peter Hall, David Jones, James Cellan Jones, Joan Littlewood, Jonathan Miller, Trevor Nunn, Robin Phillips, and Clifford Williams.

Of my own books I should mention the critical studies of *Harold Pinter* (London, 1968, 3rd edn.; 1975), *John Osborne* (London, 1968; 3rd edn., 1976), *Tom Stoppard* (London, 1977; 2nd edn., 1978), *Arnold Wesker* (London, 1970; 2nd edn., 1974), *John Whiting* (London, 1969), *John Arden* (London, 1968; 2nd edn., 1969), and *Robert Bolt* (London, 1969). *Playback* (London, 1973) contains interviews with David Storey, Peter Brook, and Terry Hands; *Playback 2* (London, 1973) with Peter Nichols and David Mercer, and a joint interview with Arnold Wesker and John Dexter. *How to Read a Play* (London, 1976) is a study of the differences between play-as-script and play-in-performance. *Artaud and After* (Oxford, 1977) contains a chapter on Artaud's influence, and *Theatre and Anti-Theatre* (London, 1979) is an account of movements since Beckett in continental and British theatre.

(Place of publication in the following list is London unless otherwise indicated.)

REFERENCE

James Vinson, ed., *Contemporary Dramatists* (London and New York, 1977)

SPECIAL ISSUES OF MAGAZINES

Tulane Drama Review, vol. II, no. 2 (Winter 1966): British Theatre 1956–66
Gambit, no. 29 (1976): Young British Dramatists issue

JOHN ARDEN

Ronald Hayman, *John Arden* (1968; 2nd edn., 1969)
Albert Hunt, *Arden: a Study of His Plays* (1974)

ROBERT BOLT

Ronald Hayman, *Robert Bolt* (1969)

EDWARD BOND

Tony Coult, *The Plays of Edward Bond* (1977)
Gambit, no. 17 (1970): Edward Bond issue

PETER BROOK

John Heilpern, *Conference of the Birds: the Story of Peter Brook in Africa* (1977)
A. C. H. Smith, *Orghast at Persepolis* (1972)
J. C. Trewin, *Peter Brook: a Biography* (1971)

T. S. ELIOT

E. Martin Browne, *The Making of T. S. Eliot's Plays* (Cambridge, 1969)
Graham Martin, ed., *Eliot in Perspective: a Symposium* (1970)
G. Smith, *Eliot's Poetry and Plays* (Chicago, 1956)

JOHN OSBORNE

Martin Banham, *Osborne* (Edinburgh, 1969)
Alan Carter, *John Osborne* (Edinburgh, 1969)
Ronald Hayman, *John Osborne* (1967; 3rd edn., 1976)
Simon Trussler, *The Plays of John Osborne* (1969)

HAROLD PINTER

Martin Esslin, *The Peopled Wound: the Plays of Harold Pinter* (1970); revised as *Pinter: a Study of His Plays* (1973)
Arthur Ganz, ed., *Pinter—a Collection of Critical Essays* (Englewood Cliffs, N.J., 1973)
Ronald Hayman, *Harold Pinter* (1968; 3rd edn., 1975)
Arnold P. Hinchliffe, *Harold Pinter* (New York, 1967)
Walter Kerr, *Harold Pinter* (New York, 1967)
Simon Trussler, *The Plays of Harold Pinter* (1973)

TOM STOPPARD

Ronald Hayman, *Tom Stoppard* (1977; 2nd edn., 1978)

ARNOLD WESKER

Ronald Hayman, *Arnold Wesker* (1970; 2nd edn., 1974)
Glenda Leeming and Simon Trussler, *The Plays of Arnold Wesker* (1971)

JOHN WHITING

Ronald Hayman, *John Whiting* (1969)
Simon Trussler, *The Plays of John Whiting* (1972)

HEATHCOTE WILLIAMS

Gambit, nos. 18–19 (1971): Heathcote Williams issue

Index